SIKH
HERITAGE

ੴ

SIKH HERITAGE
A History of Valour and Devotion

Photographs
SONDEEP SHANKAR

Text
RISHI SINGH

Foreword
HARDEEP S. PURI

Lustre Press
Roli Books

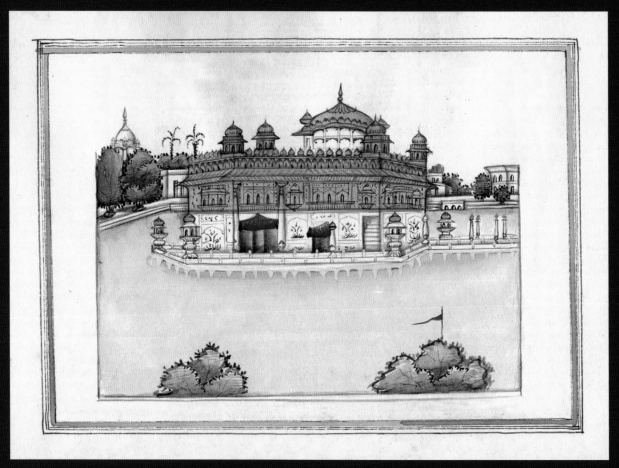

Archival sketch of Harmandir Sahib, Amritsar (courtesy Trustees of the British Museum).
PREVIOUS PAGE 2: *A painting depicting the ten Sikh Gurus from an old illustrated Bir. Guru Nanak Dev ji is seen flanked by his companions, Bala and Mardana (courtesy Maharaja Ranjit Singh Museum).*

CONTENTS

Granthis reading from the Guru Granth Sahib at Takhat Sri Hazur Sahib in Nanded, Maharashtra.

FOREWORD

An anecdote, which I came across in the book *A History of Sikhs* by Khushwant Singh many years ago remains etched in my memory to this date.

On his journey to Mecca, Guru Nanak was staying at a mosque. One night, he fell asleep with his feet pointed towards ka'bah – a gesture considered highly disrespectful. The resident priest entered the mosque to offer his morning prayers and found the Guru in this posture, ostensibly committing this act. He woke the Guru and claimed 'O servant of God, thou hast thy feet towards ka'bah, the house of God; why hast thou done such a thing?' The Guru's response was: 'Then turn my feet towards some direction where there is no God, nor the ka'bah.'

To fully understand Sikhism and the Sikh heritage, it is important to understand the origins of our faith – the questions of why, how, and in what context the birth of Sikhism took place. This requires context setting.

Hinduism witnessed a renaissance of sorts around AD 1016-1137. Prior practices and customs, which laid the foundations of a hierarchical social order based on caste, were slowly coming under the influence of the Bhakti movement. Sri Ramanuja took the philosophy of the Alvars and Adyars from southern India to the country's north. Ramananda furthered this message, and under his leadership, Hindus belonging to the lower castes were brought into the Bhakti movement.

The philosophical underpinnings of the Bhakti movement were largely a response to the spread of Islam in the country. The Indian land mass had a long-standing trade relationship with the Arab world in West Asia. The violent invasions led by Mohammed-bin-Qasim in AD 672, and by Mahmud of Ghazni from AD 971-1030, however, changed the dynamics of that relationship. The massacre of Hindus on the battlefield and the destruction of temples by Muslim invaders during those years were met by an equally strong resistance from Hindu kingdoms. And the Bhakti movement, which united all those who belonged to the Hindu faith, countered the spread of the Islamic religion in the country.

The spread of Bhakti as a response to the violent invasions was followed by the rise of a peaceful Islamic movement in India – what has today come to be described as Sufism. Pacifists from the Islamic faith who had come to India began to familiarize themselves with local religions, customs, and languages. They formed a uniquely Indian way of practising Islam, which like the Bhakti movement, focused on reciting hymns and dance, in the belief that these customs were all one needed to be one with God.

FACING PAGE: 'Ek Omkar', a symbol that represents the one supreme reality and is central to the tenets of Sikhism.
Inscribed on one of the doorways of the sanctum sanctorum of Takhat Sri Hazur Sahib, Nanded.

Another burst of violent invasion in AD 1398 by Taimur, again transformed the social and religious fabric of India. Islamic rulers came to form kingdoms, looting the traditional Hindu traders who had amassed significant wealth over the years. As a result, the peaceful coexistence of a renewed Hindu faith and a peaceful Indian version of Islam, came to a grinding halt. The practice of Hinduism reverted to its caste-dominated structures, and Islam as practiced in India focused on conversions of the so-called 'infidels'.

It was during this clash between two faiths that the birth of the first Guru, Nanak, took place. Born on 15 April 1469, Nanak from a very early age exhibited signs that would set him apart from most children his age – at the tender age of five, he began questioning the purpose of life. Not one to be bogged down by mundane activities of everyday life such as tending to cattle, Nanak would often be found in the company of holy men and ascetics.

A few years later, Nanak moved to Sultanpur, on the behest of his sister. She arranged for him to get a job as an accountant with Nawab Daulat Khan Lodhi. As mentioned earlier, Nanak always sought more from his life than the demands of a daily job. According to Janamsakhi, Nanak started organizing the singing of hymns in Sultanpur – 'every night they sang hymns… they fed everyone who came… an hour and a quarter before sunrise he would go to the river to bathe, by daylight he would be in the durbar doing his work'.

It was during one of these early morning baths by the river that Nanak had his first mystic experience. According to the Janamsakhi, in this moment, Nanak was one with God. The almighty gave Nanak a cup of *amrit* to drink and asked of him the following: 'Nanak, I am with thee. Through thee will my name be magnified. Whosoever follows thee, him will I save. Go into the world to pray and teach mankind how to pray. Be not sullied by the ways of the world. Let your life be one of praise of the word, charity, ablution, service, and prayer. Nanak, I give thee my pledge. Let this be thy life's mission.'

Guru Nanak's now famous words 'There is no Hindu, there is no Mussalman' were the result of this experience – it was all he spoke for an entire day.

The birth of Guru Nanak, and through him the religion of Sikhism, took place at a time when India was witnessing a war between two religions. Peace existed only in a vacuum – a vacuum that Guru Nanak filled through his messages of peace, which often took the form of songs, hymns, and poems.

It gives me great pride and joy to note that the practice of Sikhism today for the most part has followed in the footsteps of Guru Nanak's teachings. The idea of a peaceful and casteless society was fundamental to Guru Nanak's message – he long maintained that in the eyes of God, all humans are equal. For us Sikhs therefore there is no upper or lower caste and no person is backward. This is best exemplified in the institution we offer our prayers to God – visit any Gurdwara, and one will find people of all backgrounds and of all religions sitting together in prayer, reciting the hymns from the Guru Granth Sahib.

His message of service continues to reverberate among fellow Sikhs – the langars served in gurdwaras are cooked by members of the community and offered without religious or caste bias to all those who have come to pray. When I drive by the All India Institute of Medical Sciences in Delhi on several days of the week, I see my fellow Sikhs and other enlightened citizens from other religions, serving home-made food to those who are homeless – this is the core ethos of Sikhism, which is alive and kicking to this day.

A community, which began as a movement among farmers, over time, came to be associated with bravery in the battle zone. A traditionally peaceful religion, Sikhism faced an existential challenge when the ninth Guru, Guru Tegh Bahadur, was executed for not converting to Islam. The dominance of the Mughal Empire under the extremist Aurangzeb necessitated a response. Under the leadership of the tenth Guru, Guru Gobind Singh, the son of Guru Tegh Bahadur, a warrior community among Sikhs, referred to as the Khalsa, was born. All four of Guru Gobind Singh's sons joined him in the battle against Aurangzeb's tyrannical rule – and all four sacrificed their life to defend the egalitarian ideals of Sikhism.

The work of Sikh organizations and individuals in Syria, to provide relief to those suffering from a brutal war, is just one of many examples of their brave efforts today. While many countries in Europe, which are partly to blame for the war, are turning away refugees out of fear, Sikhs from across the world are risking their lives and working in the battle zone to uphold the highest standards of human values. Afghanistan, Yemen, and the Democratic Republic of Congo and many others have come to associate the Sikh community as one that will defend the cause of humanity, especially during the worst of times.

Sikhs are today acknowledged the world over for the professionalism and hard work they bring to their job. From leading multinational corporations to the world of academia; from government service to civil society organizations – Sikhs have excelled in all walks of life. In India, the highest offices in the land – that of the President and the Prime Minister – have been occupied by Sikhs. There are countless others who have worked towards building an India which is today held up as an example of post-colonial reconstruction – the world's fastest growing economy, and a peaceful and stable multicultural and multiethnic society.

I would like to compliment Roli Books for compiling a volume on Sikh Heritage. In the times we live in, where thanks to short attention spans, further exacerbated by social media, such a volume serves as a reminder of where Sikhism comes from, what its guiding principles state, and how it has contributed to India's secular and multicultural social fabric. Sikhs might represent just under 2 per cent of India's population, but their faith's contribution in maintaining peace in our society, and offering support to those who are most in need, is second to none.

Hardeep S. Puri

INTRODUCTION

All over the world, the Sikhs have glimmered their way to success in every field. Their religion, Sikhism, originated in the land of five rivers and is now flourishing in all continents. They have represented important political positions in Indian, North American, Canadian, Malaysian, Australian, Singaporian, British as well as Hong Kong polities to name a few. The community's extraordinary contribution in the armed forces is unique in itself. In recent times, the Sikh soldiers have represented different armies across the world. Their contributions towards science have changed the way the world connects today. Even though the Sikhs are a miniscule percentage of India's one billion population, they produce significant amount of India's food reserves; not to ignore the fact that percentage wise they are an important contributor towards India's taxes too. Worldwide, the Sikh gurdwaras feed millions of hungry men, women and children three times a day. Whether they reside in the United States of America, Canada, Australia, Malaysia, Singapore, Thailand, the United Kingdom or the African nations, they have a proven record of commitment towards that nation's development.

FACING PAGE: An archival painting depicting the sanctum sanctorum of Durbar Sahib, Amritsar (courtesy Victoria & Albert Museum).

PANORAMIC VIEW OF THE "SHIWALA" AT UMR

A panoramic view of the Durbar Sahib and parikrama around it, Harmandir Sahib, Amritsar
(courtesy Victoria & Albert Museum).

The Sikhs have been the catalysts in bringing about freedom and peace to many countries. They conquered territories and created new borders within the confines of which flourished one of the richest economies of the world. Their well-read and knowledgeable religious masters were the most travelled ones of the times, and were engaged with the political as well as religious leadership of the world. Their ideology was unique as it encompassed both the spiritual and the temporal aspects of life. Sikh masters were architects of great cities and monuments, and their far-sighted decisions brought the destitute as well as the kings to come to their doorstep for blessings. The supreme examples of sacrifice to uphold the idea of religious freedom were set by the Sikh masters and

...SUR AND SURROUNDING TANK AND BUILDINGS.

2430.

their followers. Their leadership created several splendid cities, governed the communities with justice and built their kingdoms such that the precept and practice of the idea of religious freedom faced no challenge. A new Khalsa identity to men and women was introduced on the canvas of Punjab that converted 'meek sparrows to hawks'!

ENGAGING WITH SIKH HERITAGE

Heritage is the entire collection of quantifiable symbols handed on by the past to each society and therefore, to the whole of humankind, acting as a major link with history. It is the storehouse of a society's experience that binds it with a context of its inheritance. The understanding of the body of 'heritage' could thus be inclusive of various forms of memories such as archival material including single items, cultural objects, fine arts, machinery along with apparatus and artefacts.

It is important to recognize the origin and context in establishing the story of the Sikh historic objects and buildings, as there is a risk that some of the objects may have been lost or may lose their story with time. The primary reason behind such a loss is today's fast-paced lifestyle and rapid urbanization. This book endeavours to contextually depict the various facets of these heritage objects related to the ten Gurus, and leads ultimately to the dynamic nature of Punjab's cultural expression. It attempts to capture the evolution of the Harmandir Sahib in the city of Amritsar – the intricate engravings on the dome and walls have been captured in detail. The style practised by the photographer has created a feeling of candid curiosity as the reader contemplates the divine experience that the Harmandir Sahib offers. We engage with the temporal seats of the Sikhs – the *takhats*. The images that go along with the narrative have beautifully captured the *takhats* and the people, thus portraying a relationship between the vibrant history. There are many things that have been left behind with families and institutions. These are generally clothes, weapons, and belongings associated with the Gurus and important Sikh personalities. Through these objects, association of a family with Gurus is established, as they mark past events. These objects could also be symbolic in defining the Guru's blessings over the family who possess these objects or historic sites. These are spread all over India and Pakistan in museums, government ownership, and private collections around the world – some of them well cared for, while some of them completely ignored.

This new approach aims at the conception of Sikh heritage not only as the sacred masterpieces of the past to be valued and conserved, but also as emblematic and living spaces to be appropriated by the local communities, who are the bearers of a rich and active collective memory. This work is the photographic documentation of the consequences of a longer and more complex process stimulated by a re-examination of the overall idea of Sikh heritage. Furthermore, an effort has been made to consider the Sikh historicity through objects both in time and space. An effort has been made to document some of the historical places that survived the devastation through the acts of Man or God.

The book endeavours to take one on a journey to gain an understanding of the very idea of Sikh history.

FACING PAGE: Devotees paying obeisance to Guru Granth Sahib at Harmandir sahib.

19

ABOVE: An illustrated folio from a handwritten Guru Granth Sahib. The Holy Granth is written in Gurmukhi script. Literally meaning 'from the Guru's mouth', Gurmukhi was standardized by the second Sikh Guru, Guru Angad Dev.

LEFT: The holy book of the Sikhs, Guru Granth Sahib, was first installed in the Harmandir Sahib's sanctum sanctorum on Bhandon Sudi 1, 1661 BK (16 August 1604). Baba Budha, one of the most venerated and earliest disciples of Guru Nanak, who applied the 'tilak of Guruship' to the five Gurus, carried the holy book on his head. Guru Arjan Dev walked behind the holy book, swinging the whisk over it as a mark of utmost respect. The day was marked with the singing of Shabad Kirtan. Baba Budha was the first priest of the Harmandir Sahib. This image marks the historic day when installation of the Holy Granth took place. The Granth is brought out once a year on a golden palanquin, with devotees doing parikrama around the sarovar *that surrounds the sanctum.*

CHAPTER I

EMERGENCE
OF THE SIKH FAITH

PUNJAB, THE LAND OF FIVE RIVERS, IS WHERE CIVILIZATIONS HAVE FLOURISHED SINCE THE DAWN OF HISTORY. ON THE CANVAS OF SOUTH ASIAN HISTORY, THE FIFTEENTH CENTURY INTRODUCED A NEW ERA — ON ONE SIDE THE EMERGENCE OF THE GREATEST EMPIRE OF THE MUGHALS AND ON THE OTHER, WORLD'S NEWEST RELIGION, SIKHISM, TOOK FORM. ONE HAD LAID ITS FOUNDATIONS ON ITS TEMPORAL STRENGTH AND THE OTHER ON ITS SPIRITUAL STRENGTH.

FACING PAGE: Founder of Sikhism, Guru Nanak's image inscribed on one of the doorways of the sanctum sanctorum of Takhat Sri Hazur Sahib, Nanded.
FOLLOWING PAGES 22-23: A large series of paintings unfold, stage by stage, the life of Guru Nanak on the interior walls of the first floor of Gurdwara Baba Atal, a nine-storey octagonal tower not too far from the Golden Temple. Originally a samadhi of Baba Atal Rai, the son of Guru Hargobind, the sixth Sikh Guru, it was transformed, with the passage of time, into a nine-storey gurdwara, in memory of the nine years of Baba Atal. These murals date back to the early nineteenth century.

LEFT TO RIGHT: Gurdwara Janam Asthan, Nankana Sahib, Pakistan. Situated around 48 miles west of Lahore, Guru Nanak was born here, earlier known as Rai Bhoi Di Talwandi. After the birth of Guru Nanak, it began to be known as Nankana Sahib; Gurdwara Tambu Sahib, Pakistan; and Gurdwara Mal ji Sahib, Nankana Sahib, Pakistan.

number of his followers. He travelled to far off lands, carrying the divine message revealed to him. He was accompanied by Bhai Mardana, his rebeck player. These journeys that Nanak undertook are known as Odysseys, or *Udasis*. He tried to visit the holy places of all the Indian religions en route, especially on the occasions of festivities at those sites. He witnessed the rituals, engaged with the spiritual leaders and guided the followers according to his own understanding. He stopped at Kurukshetra during solar eclipse, an important occasion when a large number of Hindus come together to take a holy dip. Afterwards through Panipat and Delhi he reached Haridwar – one of the most important religious destinations for Hindus, on the banks of River Ganga. He engaged with a number of pilgrims who were pouring water towards the sun as a ritual. Guru Nanak performed the same ritual in a different manner by pouring water in the other direction. The other devotees gathered there were surprised and asked him the reason for this action. He replied, 'If you can make the water reach the sun, many millions of miles away, mine will surely reach my fields in Punjab, only a few hundred miles away.'

Nanak, who had been acknowledged as a Guru by now, acquired many followers during his journeys. After Haridwar, he reached Benaras (Varanasi), an important intellectual centre of the Hindus, on the occasion of *Shivaratri*. There he engaged with Chatur Das in a religious discourse, who subsequently became his follower and spread the word of Nanak. From there, Nanak travelled to Gaya and Patna where a jeweller, named Salis Rai, became his follower and shared his message with people. From Patna, Guru Nanak travelled to Assam and then to Dacca along with Mardana. On his return, he visited Cuttack, where now stands Gurdwara Datan Sahib. At the Jagannath Temple in Puri, one of the holiest places for the Hindus, Nanak, instead of joining the *aarti* along with the congregation in front of deities (idols), began singing the *aarti* he had himself composed, thus revealing his message to all those present in his unique way.

The Guru began his second journey, but just before doing so, he established a new town, on a piece of land offered by a disciple named Karori of Lahore. He established the town of Kartarpur there. He travelled south, where his visits have been marked with gurdwaras all over the Indian peninsula as far as Ceylon. He met Shivnabh of Jaffna in Ceylon, who had earlier been introduced to the ideals of Nanak by the merchant Mansukh.

The Guru's next odyssey was towards the north. He met Gorakhnath yogis at Gorakhamata in the Himalayas, while travelling with Hassu, a blacksmith and Sihan, a washerman. The place is now known as Nanakmata. Subsequently, Nanak travelled further north to Tibet and Nepal and visited the famous Mansarovar lake, and on his way back, returned through Leh, where he rested at a place now known as Pathar Sahib. He further reached Punjab via Srinagar.

His fourth odyssey took him to the west. Accompanied by Mardana, he travelled to Mecca, the most revered place for the Muslims, where he went to sleep with his feet directed towards the holy shrine. This was objected to by a man who along with others was annoyed at what he saw, and told Nanak that his feet were pointing towards the abode of God, to which Nanak replied, 'Turn my feet where God is not.' The message was well taken by those present. On his return to Punjab via Baghdad and Persia, he witnessed the sacking of Saaidpur by Babur – a beginning of a new era in Indian subcontinent's polity.

After several years of travelling, Guru Nanak settled down at Kartarpur as a farmer. His followers were the first Sikhs of an Order that was to prevail for many years to come. For these Sikhs, Guru Nanak needed a leader who had been through all the tests of becoming an ideal Sikh. He chose Guru Angad and proclaimed him to be the next Guru for the Sikhs. On 7 September 1539, Guru Nanak left the world.

28

FROM LEFT TO RIGHT: *Gurdwara Panja Sahib, Pakistan. Guru Nanak's palm imprint on a rock, Panja Sahib.*
FACING PAGE: *A painting depicting Guru Nanak Dev ji holding the rock.*

30

Gurdwara Patthar (Pith) Sahib, Ladakh. While in Leh Guru Nanak came to be revered as Nanak Lama. According to a local legend, once a demon in the area used to terrorize people. One morning when the Guru was sitting in meditation, the demon pushed a large boulder down a hilltop, with the intention of killing the Guru. The boulder gained speed as it rumbled down the hillside, but when it touched the Guru's body, it softened like warm wax and came to a halt against Guru Nanak's back. Thinking that the Guru had been killed, the demon came down and was taken aback to see him deep in meditation. In a fit of anger, he tried to push the boulder with his right foot, but his foot got embedded into the rock, leaving an imprssion of it in the rock. Pulling his foot from the boulder, the demon was dumfounded to see the impression his foot had just left in the stone. He fell at the feet of Guru Nanak and begged forgiveness. Guru Sahib advised him to give up his evil deeds and to serve people. This changed the life of the demon, who gave up evil deeds and started serving the people.

Sacred chola, *or cloak, of Guru Nanak Dev. This* chola *was believed to be presented to the Guru during his visit to Mecca by a Muslim saint in Baghdad. The chola has verses from the holy Koran embroidered on it. At Mecca, Guru Nanak was reproached for sleeping with his feet to the east – towards the holy Kaaba – by a local mullah. Guru Nanak asked the mullah to move his feet to the direction where there is no God to stress the point that God is omnipresent.*

A sevadar *showing Baba Rup Chand's topi at Gurdwara Manji Sahib at Kartarpur. The gurdwara was once the house of Guru Har Rai's daughter, Bibi Rup Kaur, who was presented the topi in her dowry.*

32

ਇਹ ਚੌਖਟਾ ਗੁਰਦਵਾਰਾ ਸਾਹਿਬ
ੇ ਨੀਂਹ ਦੀ ਖੁਦਾਈ ਦੇ ਵੇਲੇ
ਮੀਨ ਵਿਚੋਂ ਨਿਕਲੀਆਂ ਸਨ ।

33

Gurdwara Baoli Sahib in Pehowa, Kurukshetra, is dedicated to the memory of Guru Nanak Dev's visit to the town. At the time of the Guru's visit, the local pandits enjoyed absolute command over the locals. These pandits made a gold earring as big as a chariot wheel and threw it into the Saraswati River. They asked the locals for donations for the gold earring. The following day they presented to the locals how their offerings had multiplied during the night. Such deceitful acts of the pandits made people donate even more. When Guru Nanak gained knowledge of these fraudulent tricks of the pandits, he admonished them and remarked that while the gains from public offerings had multiplied, the sins of the pandits would multiply even further in the same way. The pandits sought forgiveness from the Guru.

34

An illustrated pothi, believed to be of Guru Nanak Dev ji, has been handed down to the Pothimala family at Village Guru Harsahai.
FACING PAGE: A painting in the Pothimala building, founded by Guru Jeewan Mal, seventh direct descendant of the fourth Sikh Guru Ram Das.

GURU ANGAD DEV

1504–1552

Guru Angad, previously known as Lehna, was the son of Daya Kaur and Bhai Pheru – a businessman of Matte di Sarai, a place near Muktsar. Lehna was an ardent follower of the Hindu Goddess Durga, and led pilgrims to Sri Jawalamukhi every year. During one of his journeys, Lehna stopped at Kartarpur to meet Guru Nanak and within no time decided to dedicate his life to the philosophy of the Guru. Guru Nanak, after being assured of his genuine and absolute dedication, nominated Lehna as his successor on 13 June 1539, identifying him as Guru Angad.

Guru Angad shifted his base to Khadur Sahib and continued to perform all the tasks that Guru Nanak had begun, specially the practice of langar, which continued for the whole day and was looked after by his wife – Mata Khivi. After his early morning prayers, he tended to the sick and in the afternoon, he took a personal interest in teaching young children the

37

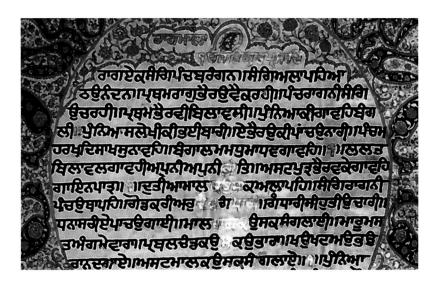

Guru Angad Dev standardized the Gurmukhi script of the Punjabi language. The script was taught by the Guru himself to his Sikhs. Soon the script became the script of the people of Punjab. FACING PAGE: Sri Guru Angad (1504–1552). Painting from Baoli Sahib, Goindwal.

Gurmukhi letters, and also encouraged them to wrestle. He even organized matches at the *Mal Akhara*. His most important contribution was to record Guru Nanak's wisdom in the Gurmukhi script. Thus, it was due to him that *Gurbani* became the nucleus of the Sikh faith. Guru Angad passed away on 29 March 1552. In Khadur Sahib, there are many gurdwaras that mark the incidents of the Guru's life.

Guru Angad observed the traits of an ideal Sikh in Amardas (1479–1574), who was born in the Bhalla Khatri family in Basarke, Amritsar. He was a staunch Vaishnavite and regularly paid obeisance to the River Ganga at Haridwar. One morning, Amardas heard the hymns of Guru Nanak, sung by the daughter of Guru Angad, Bibi Amro – who was in turn married to his brother's son. Mesmerized by the magic of *Gurbani*, Amardas devoted his life henceforth to Guru Angad for twelve years. With utmost dedication and submission, rain or shine, he used to get water from the Beas River for the Guru's bath in the wee hours of every morning. Observing, testing and acknowledging that Amardas had proved himself to be a true disciple or believer of the Guru, he was bestowed with the honour to lead the Sikhs.

A Nihang Sikh preparing langar. FACING PAGE: *Guru Angad Dev maintained and developed the institution of langar. The Guru's wife, Mata Khivi, personally worked in the kitchen and served food to the followers and visitors. Her devotion to langar finds mention in the Guru Granth Sahib.*

GURU AMARDAS

1479–1574

Guru Amardas moved his base to Goindwal – a town that lies on the road connecting Delhi and Lahore. He contributed by encouraging the Sikhs to lead a life of domesticity and shun asceticism. During the times of the third Guru, Goindwal became a big centre and many Hindus and Muslims began coming to meet the Guru. A big *baoli* (stepwell), with 84 steps, was constructed for the devotees. It was also during this time that langar emerged as the epitome of the Sikh ethos. Emperor Akbar was so impressed by the magnitude of the institute of langar that he offered to make a contribution to it, however, which was refused by Guru Amardas. He was also instrumental in eradicating the practice of Sati in Punjab and was in opposition to the practice of purdah. As the number of Sikhs had increased, an elaborate system was created by the Guru known as *manjis*, each being led by a Sikh devotee – male or female. The Guru also structured the marriage and death ceremonies for the new community. All the ceremonies would now be performed using the *Gurbani*. He breathed his last on 1 September 1574 after consecrating his son-in-law, Ramdas, as his successor.

41

ABOVE: Sacred hair and chola *of Guru Amar Das ji at Gurdwara Sri Chaubara Sahib, Goindwal.*
FACING PAGE: Sri Guru Amar Das (1504–1552). Painting from Baoli Sahib, Goindwal.

42

ABOVE LEFT: Kesh, *strands of hair of Guru Amar Das preserved in Gurdwara Chaubara Sahib, Goindwal.*

ABOVE RIGHT: The Baoli Sahib is an open well 8 metres across, paved with 84 steps, at Goindwal. It is a popular belief that by reciting Japji Sahib, bani *of Guru Nanak Dev, at each of the 84 steps provides* moksha, *or liberation from 84,00,000 cycles of birth and death.*

LEFT: This historic gilded killi, *a wooden peg, is stuck in the wall of Gurdwara Chaubara Sahib at Goindwal. It is believed that Guru Amar Das used to meditate standing, holding this* killi.

Gurdwara Khadoor Sahib, Killa Sahib: Sri Amar Das used to fetch water from the River Beas at Goindwal for the sacred bath of Guru Angad Dev for twelve years. One day, Sri Amar Das fell striking against the peg of a weaver. On hearing the noise, the weaver's wife spoke ill for Sri Amar Das, for which it is believed that she became mad. It is believed that with the touch of Guru Angad Dev, the peg turned green and grew into a full-grown Kareer tree. With time, the tree dried up and has been preserved in a frame for the devotees to pay their tributes. It was here that Baba Budha ji blessed Shri Amar Das to become the Guru.

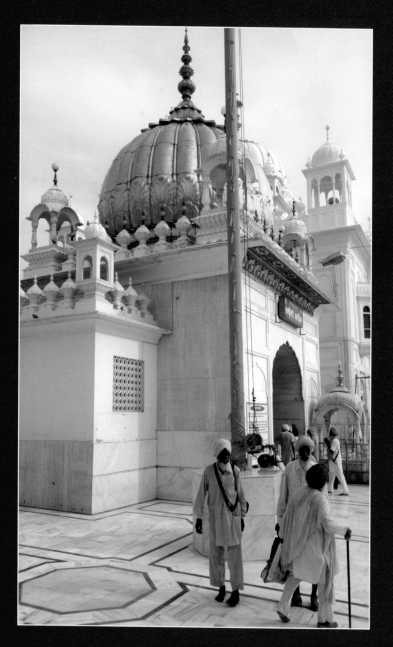

ਥੰਮ ਸਾਹਿਬ ਤੇ ਚੁੱਲਾ ਸਾਹਿਬ ਬੀਬੀ ਭਾਨੀ ਜੀ
ਇਸ ਥੰਮ ਨਾਲ ਸ੍ਰੀ ਗੁਰੂ ਅਰਜਨ ਦੇਵ ਜੀ
ਛੋਟੀ ਅਵਸਥਾ ਵਿੱਚ ਖੇਡਿਆ ਕਰਦੇ ਸਨ
ਅਤੇ ਬੀਬੀ ਭਾਨੀ ਜੀ ਏਥੇ ਪ੍ਰਸ਼ਾਦੇ ਤਿਆਰ
ਕਰਕੇ ਸੰਗਤਾਂ ਨੂੰ ਛਕਾਂਦੇ ਸੀ

LEFT: *View of Gurdwara Baoli Saheb, Goindwal.*
RIGHT: *Gurdwara Tham Sahib and Chullah Sahib, Bibi Bhani ji, Goindwal. Guru Arjan Dev ji during his younger days played along with this Tham, and Bibi Bhani cooked food and served the Sikh sangat.*

LEFT: *Gurdwara Chaubara Sahib, Goindwal.*
RIGHT: *Old bricks now covered with plaster showcased at Guru Arjun Dev's birth place in Goindwal.*

GURU RAMDAS

1534–1581

Guru Ramdas, originally known as Jetha, was born in a Sodhi family in Chuna Mandi, Lahore, on 24 September 1534. He worked devotedly with the other Sikhs on the stepwell at Goindwal. Guru Amar Das noticed Jetha's respectful disposition and married his daughter, Bibi Bhani, to him. Before Guru Amar Das left for heavenly abode, he nominated Jetha, who was later known as Ramdas, as the next Guru.

Guru Ramdas took many steps that gave new direction to the community. He purchased 500 bighas of land on the payment of Rs. 700 *akbari* to the owners – the zamindars of Tung – to establish a new centre for the Sikhs. Hence was laid the foundation of one of the most important cities of the world – Amritsar, 40 kilometres from Goindwal. The pool of water that surrounds the Harmandir Sahib was also constructed by Guru Ramdas. He encouraged entrepreneurship and asked all the Sikhs to support the one who is starting a business. As many as 52 businessmen were encouraged to settle in the city. He established a wide network of *masands*, or representatives of the Guru, who collected contributions from the Sikhs living far away. The Guru was a divinely inspired poet and a composer par excellence. The Guru Granth Sahib contains 638 hymns in 30 different ragas composed by him. Guru Ramdas died on 1 September 1581, leaving the reigns of Sikhism in the hands of Guru Arjan (1563–1606), his youngest son.

FACING PAGE: Sri Guru Ramdas (1534–1581). Painting from Baoli Sahib, Goindwal.

LEFT AND ABOVE: *Archival photographs of the Harmandir Sahib, Amritsar (courtesy of the Getty's Open Content Program and Private Collection).*

50

Archival photograph of Darshani Deorhi, c. 1900–1906 (courtesy Getty Images).

51

Darshani Deorhi as it looks presently: Darshani Deorhi is the extravagantly ornamented main entrance leading to the pathway to Harmandir Sahib. The archway under the Darshani Deorhi was embellished with sheets of gilded copper by Sangat Singh, the Raja of Jind. Almost every Sikh chief of Punjab has contributed to its architectural embellishments from time to time.

FIFTH GURU
GURU ARJAN DEV
1563–1606

Guru Arjan was born on 15 April 1563 and was the youngest son of Guru Ramdas. He took residence at Chak Ramdas and completed the tasks started by his father in order to tie the Sikhs into a cohesive community. Prominent institutions such as the institutions of *dasvandh* (1/10th of income of a Sikh to be donated for the benefit of the community) and *masands* (representatives of the Gurus – one of their tasks was to collect *dasvandh*) were established by Guru Arjan. He laid the foundation of the central temple, the Harmandir Sahib, in the middle of the *sarovar* that was constructed by Guru Ramdas.

Guru Arjan also founded the cities of Tarn Taran and Kartarpur, in the Jullandar Doab. The lepers were treated by the Guru and his Sikhs compassionately in the city of Tarn Taran. He also constructed the stepwell at the Dabbi Bazaar in Lahore that helped many overcome the famine that had engulfed the Punjab at the time.

The most significant contribution made by Guru Arjan was the compilation of the Granth. The Guru brought the pothi sahib, manuscript of writings of the previous Gurus from Bhai Mohan in Goindwal, and at Ramsar, began his work of composition and compilation. Besides his own and that of the Gurus, he included the *bani* of several Hindu and Muslim saints, mainly Kabir, Farid, Namdev, Ravidas, Jaidev, Trilochan, Ramanand, Sadhna, Beni, Surdas, Bhikhan, Bhai Mardana, Dhanna, Pipa, Sen, Parmanand, etc. – most of whom belonged to the marginalized castes. The Granth was prepared by Guru Arjan with Bhai Gurdas as its calligrapher. It is arranged

A wall painting at Takhat Hazur Sahib depicting Mata Ganga, wife of Guru Arjun Dev, seeking blessings from Baba Budha, one of the earliest disciples of Guru Nanak. He performed the formal coronation of five Sikh Gurus.
FACING PAGE: Sri Guru Arjan (1504–1552). Painting from Baoli Sahib, Goindwal.

according to thirty-one musical measures, and the passages are arranged according to a subject or thought with groups of hymns forming single paragraphs, always beginning with an invocation to God. While the book was still in the making, there was a complaint filed in Akbar's court against the Guru about certain matter being included in the book. Emperor Akbar visited the Guru at Goindwal, and was so pleased to hear some of the passages from the Granth read out to him that he remitted a portion of the year's revenue to the zamindars of Goindwal.

When Jahangir took over the Mughal Empire after Emperor Akbar's death, he wanted to discourage the spread of any other faith. During his struggle for the Mughal throne, he fought with his brother Khusrau, who was helped by the Guru. The Guru was arrested by the orders of Jahangir and on his way to Lahore was handed over to Chandu Shah, who it is believed carried a personal grudge against the Guru. At Lahore, he was subjected to all sorts of tortures in the summer heat of Punjab, and was then thrown into the cold water of River Ravi. He was succeeded by his son Hargobind.

54

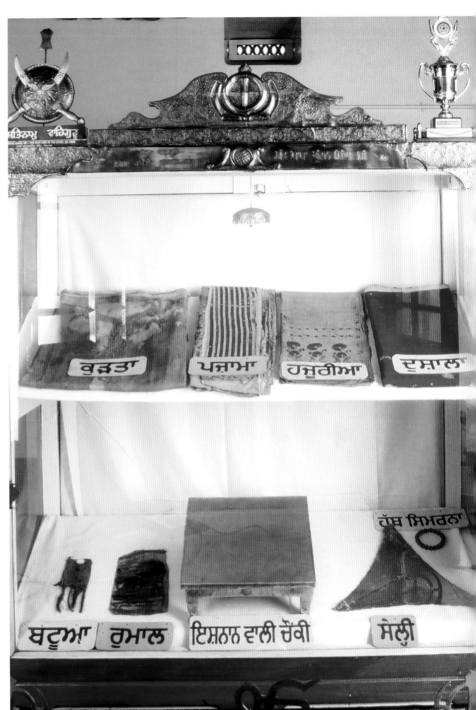

ਕੁੜਤਾ ਪਜਾਮਾ ਹਜੂਰੀਆ ਦੁਸ਼ਾਲ

ਦੱਬ ਸਿਮਰਨਾ

ਬਟੂਆ ਰੁਮਾਲ ਇਸ਼ਨਾਨ ਵਾਲੀ ਚੌਕੀ ਸੇਲੀ

Gurdwara Chheharta Sahib is named after a well that Guru Arjan had constructed. The well has six Persian wheels installed that could operate simultaneously, hence its name, Chheharta, which means 'having six wheels'.
RIGHT: *Relics of the Guru preserved at Gurdwara Panjvi Padshahi, Bilga village. These are the Guru's kurta, pyjama, hazuria, dushala, purse, handkerchief, seat and simama, and a silk head cover.*
FACING PAGE: *Shrine of Ath Sath Tirath in Golden Temple complex near Dukh Bhanjani Beri. It is a raised marble platform, which is the Ath Sath Tirath, the place of the sixty-eight Holy Places. It is believed that taking bath here can fulfill one's desire to visit sixty-eight sacred shrines in India.*

GURU HARGOBIND

1595–1644

Guru Hargobind changed the role of the Guru for the Sikhs by expressing his philosophy of wearing two swords, representing two facets of Sikhism – *miri* (temporality) and *piri* (spirituality). This change came as an addition to the Sikh ethos whose time, perhaps, had come. He was only eleven years old when he became the Guru. He was trained by Baba Budha Ji, who taught him the art of weaponry and about the challenges that he might face as a Guru. For the first time, not only did the house of the Gurus move towards the construction of forts by building the fort of Lohgarh in Amritsar, but it also dispensed justice resolving the issues of the common man in front of the Akal Takhat. Moreover, 500 Sikhs came forward to volunteer for the Guru's army without any remuneration.

Emperor Jahangir did not remain untouched by the activities associated with the Sikhs. He arrested Guru Hargobind and put him in the Gwalior prison along with many other ruling elites. As the news of the arrest spread, people began flocking to the fort and pleaded for his release. The pressure built by the Guru's followers and supporters led Jahangir to let go of the Guru; but he refused to be released until the other 52 princes in the prison were set free too. It is believed that the permission was granted subject to the fact that only those who could hold onto the Guru's dress, would be released. The Guru acquired a customized dress with 52 ends; each prince held onto one and was set free. It is because of this incident that Guru Hargobind is also known as *Bandi chorr*, or a person who frees people.

Guru Hargobind journeyed outside Punjab, travelling as far as Kashmir in the north and Pilibhit in the east, inspiring people to follow Sikhism. Shah Jahan succeeded Emperor Jahangir, and his policies led to the demolition of the religious places of the non-Muslims. The action taken by the Mughal authority came in conflict with those of the Sikhs, resulting in battles between the two factions. These battles were fought under the leadership of the Guru. Won by the Sikhs, they brought a new dimension in the polity of Punjab, as they set an example where tyranny by the Mughals could be overcome. The Guru retired to Kiratpur and spent the last ten years of his life in meditation and prayer. He appointed Har Rai, his grandson, as his successor and died on 3 March 1644.

FACING PAGE: Sri Guru Hargobind (1595–1644). Painting from Baoli Sahib, Goindwal.

58

Bagrian is located on Nabha–Malerkotla road in the Sangrur district of Punjab.
FACING PAGE: Karchas *(large spoons) and a tawa (iron plate/griddle) used by Guru Hargobind and Guru Gobind*
Singh, presented to Bhai Roop Chand of Bagrian family. The Bagrian family is the continuation of a tradition of
religious service from the times of Bhai Rup Chand, who was blessed by Guru Hargobind.

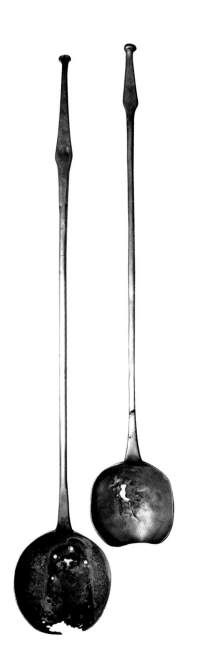

60

Weapons at Akal Takhat.
RIGHT, *ABOVE AND BELOW: A priest in the Akal Takhat in the Golden Temple complex, Amritsar, displaying two historic swords – Miri (left) and Piri (right) – of the sixth Guru Hargobind ji. Propounding the philosophy of connection between spiritual and temporal matters, Guru Hargobind ji established Akal Takhat, the seat of Sikh temporal authority.*

FACING PAGE, *ABOVE: Simarana of Guru Hargobind, from the collection of the Sangha family of Drolli Bhai Ki.*
BELOW: *A miniature Guru Granth Sahib given to the Sikh soldiers during the Second World War (courtesy of the Dalla family).*

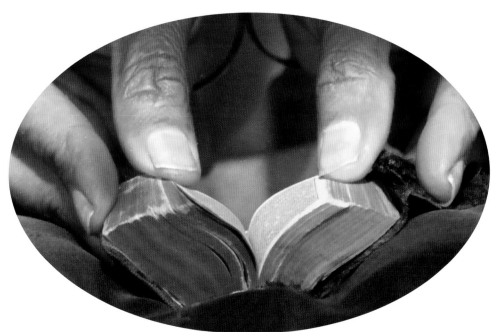

63

FACING PAGE AND ABOVE: Belongings of Guru Hargobind from the Sangha family of Drolli Bhai Ki Collection. Gagar *(facing page)*, ganga sagar *(left)*, tabalbaz *(right, below)*, jhama *or scrub (right, above)*.

GURU HAR RAI

1630–1661

Guru Har Rai, born in Kiratpur on 16 January 1630, was the son of Baba Gurditta, and the grandson of Guru Hargobind. He was the best example of a leader who imbibed the ethos of *miri* and *piri* in life, as demonstrated by the fact that he was not only trained in the art of weaponry but was also well versed in the spiritual way of life as propounded by Guru Nanak. Guru Har Rai kept a strong army of 2,200 horsemen who were ever ready to be deployed at a short notice. Furthermore, he established institutions for the spread of Sikhism – Bhagat Bhagwan established centres in Eastern India, Bhai Pheru preached in Rajasthan and Southern Punjab, Bhai Gonda was sent to Kabul, Bhai Natha to Dhaka, and Bhai Jodh to Multan. The families of Bagrian and Kaithal preached in the Malwa region.

During the struggle for the Mughal throne after Shah Jahan's death, Dara Shikoh was assisted by the Guru at Goindwal. Consequently, after Dara Shikoh's loss and Aurangzeb's ascension to the throne, the king summoned the Guru to his court, in response to which the Guru sent his son – Ram Rai. It is believed that Ram Rai misinterpreted a hymn from the Holy Granth to please Aurangzeb. As a consequence of Ram Rai's act, the emperor bestowed upon him a *jagir* in the Doon valley. The Guru died on 6 October 1661, naming Harkishan as his successor.

65

A historic manji, *or cot, at Gurdwara Manji Sahib, Kiratpur marks the site where Guru Hargobind's daughter, Bibi Veero, lived. A sacred book containing hymns from the* bani *(pothi), a cot, a hand fan, and a scarf (gifted to her by her father) and the head cover of Guru Nanak Dev are kept here.*
FACING PAGE: Sri Guru Har Rai (1630–1661). Painting from Baoli Sahib, Goindwal.

GURU HARKISHAN

1656–1664

Guru Harkishan, who was just over five years old when he became the Guru, was the younger son of Guru Har Rai and Mata Sulakhni. The fact that Ram Rai was hoping to become the Guru led to a struggle between him and those who believed that Guru Harkishan was the real Guru. Ram Rai protested to the Mughal emperor in Delhi, claiming his right over the House of the Guru. Mirza Jai Singh, who was the devotee of the Gurus, and also a confidante of the Mughal emperor, invited Guru Harkishan to his bungalow in Raisina, Delhi. Guru Harkishan was seized with high fever, which was followed by small pox – prevalent at that time in Delhi. Just before he left for his heavenly abode, he uttered the words 'Baba Bakala', indicating that his successor would be found in Bakala.

67

Gurdwara of Sri Guru Amar Das Ate Guru Har Rai Sahib at the ancient town of Kurukshetra, Haryana. Kurukshetra once extended beyond town to a region corresponding roughly to the central and western parts of the state of Haryana and southern Punjab.
FACING PAGE: Sri Guru Harkishan (1656–1664). Painting from Baoli Sahib, Goindwal.

Gurdwara Sri Bangla Sahib in New Delhi marks the place of the stay of the eighth Sikh Guru Harkrishan ji. The Guru came to Delhi at the behest of Mughal Emperor Aurangzeb. Raja Jai Singh invited Guru ji to the present site, which originally belonged to the raja. The raja's wife thought of testing the spiritual powers of the Guru ji and disguised herself as a maid servant and sat among the attendants. Guru ji, all of 8 years, recognized the queen and sat in her lap, thus convincing her. In those days, small pox epidemic was spreading through Delhi. The citizens of Delhi suffered grief and death. It is believed that with the blessings of the Guru, the people of Delhi were saved from the epidemic.

GURU TEGH BAHADUR
1621–1675

Guru Tegh Bahadur, the youngest son of Guru Hargobind, was born at Guru ke Mahal in the city of Amritsar on 1 April 1621. He went to live in Bakala after the death of his father. It was for this place that the proclamation was made by Guru Harkishan in Delhi. At Bakala, many pretended to be the future Guru, but it was Makhan Shah Lubana, who was a trader by profession, who discovered that Tegh Bahadur was the Guru of the Sikhs.

The Guru took the message of Sikhism to various parts of the Indian subcontinent. He travelled east, visiting Agra, Allahabad, Benaras, Sasaram, Gaya, and Patna and settled his family at Patna, since his wife, Mata Gujri was expecting. Wherever he went, he met with the Sikh *sangat*, and re-enforced the ideals of Sikhism. The *sangats* were encouraged to serve humanity and there are *hukamnamas* that reflect this synergy between the Guru and his *sangat*. After his departure from Monghyr, he wrote a letter to the *sangat* of Patna, informing them that he was going further towards Assam and that they should find and provide a comfortable home for his family in the city. The news of his son's birth on 22 December 1666 reached him when he was in Dacca. His trust in the *sangat* of Patna was immense, as he continued his journey in the service of his *sangat* in eastern India. He also travelled to Assam where a gurdwara marks his visit. On his return, he found the people terrorized by the religious conversions that were common during the rule of Aurangzeb. He called for his family and met with his son, Gobind Das, who at a very young age, had begun to show signs of someone who realized the values preserved in the doctrines laid down by Guru Nanak. This is clearly demonstrated by the following incident: One day, after the visit of Kashmiri Pundits, Guru Tegh Bahadur was lost in thought. When young Gobind Rai asked him the reason for being in such a state, the Guru replied that the world was facing difficult times, and the only way to resolve it was the sacrifice of a great soul. In the blink of an eye, young Gobind said that there could not be a soul greater than you!

FACING PAGE: Sri Guru Tegh Bahadur (1621–1675). Painting from Baoli Sahib, Goindwal.

With his belief *'Frighten not and Fear not'*, the ninth Guru began his journey to Delhi. At Saifabad, near the state of Patiala, Saifuddin, the Nawab, waited for his arrival and also had a gurdwara constructed in the fort. Sadly enough, many of his masands distanced themselves from him for the fear of atrocities from the authorities. He was arrested in Agra, and brought to Delhi where he was asked to embrace Islam. In front of him, his two companions Mati Das and Sati Das were executed and the Guru himself was beheaded publicly on 11 November 1675 at Chandni Chowk in Delhi. Before this ordeal, he had bestowed the rights of the Guru to Gobind Rai.

72

ABOVE: Kharawan, *wooden sandals of Guru Tegh Bahadur at Patna Sahib.*
LEFT: Sword of Guru Tegh Bahadur inscribed with the words 'Guru Teg Bahadur, Azam Abaad' in Arabic script. From the Collection of Maharaja of Patiala at Moti Bagh Palace.

Gurdwara Sis Ganj in Chandni Chowk is one of the nine historical gurdwaras in Delhi. It was the site where the ninth Guru Tegh Bahadur was beheaded on the orders of the Mughal Emperor Aurangzeb in 1675 for refusing to convert to Islam. The gurdwara was first constructed in 1783 by Baghel Singh, a Sikh military leader to commemorate the martyrdom site of the Sikh Guru. The trunk of the tree beneath which the head of the Guru was severed and the well used by him for taking bath during his imprisonment, have been preserved in the gurdwara.

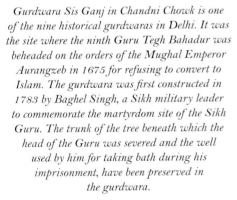

TENTH GURU
GURU GOBIND SINGH
1666–1708

Gobind Rai was only nine years old when his father was killed in Delhi. He was in the most difficult of situations politically, personally, and emotionally. The headless body of Guru Tegh Bahadur was taken by a Sikh outside the city to his home and burnt entirely for the purpose of cremation – this site is now marked by Gurdwara Rakab Ganj. A Rangretta Sikh – by the name of Jaita – took the head of Guru Tegh Bahadur Singh to Guru Gobind at Anandpur, where it was cremated.

Guru Gobind was formally installed as Guru on 29 March 1676. In 1685, Guru Gobind shifted to Nahan in the foothills of the Himalayas and settled at Paonta Sahib, on the banks of River Jamuna. Here he equipped himself in various languages and also studied history and world religions. The time spent at Paonta Sahib can be credited for shaping the course of Sikh history to a considerable extent. Apart from making it one of the most prolific phases for the Sikhs in intercultural understanding, this phase is probably also credited for the creation of the Khalsa. All the Sikhs engaged themselves in hunting, riding, swimming, archery and sword play; and this regimented routine empowered them to a great degree. Fateh Chand of Garwal felt threatened due to the activities of the Sikhs and attacked the Guru preemptively. At that time 500 pathans deserted him, adversely affecting his martial strength and yet, the Guru, for his better war tactics, won this battle at Bhangani in 1688.

The Guru, soon after the battle of Bhangani, returned to Anandpur, where he built four forts – Anandgarh, Lohgarh, Keshgarh and Fatehgarh – to keep the hill states in check. The mission of the Guru had not reached its epitome yet – the unique act that was to change the course of history had yet to transpire. On the day of Baisakh, 30 March 1699, he called a large gathering of all the Sikhs at Anandpur. This gathering was to witness the birth of the Khalsa. Going beyond any precedent, the master bowed down before his newly formed baptized students, and got baptized himself. The five symbols of the Khalsa – unshorn hair (*kes*), a comb (*kangha*), a pair of shorts (*kachha*), an iron bracelet (*kara*), and a sword (*kirpan*) – were to be worn at all times by members of the Khalsa panth.

FACING PAGE: Sri Guru Gobind Singh (1666–1708). Painting from Baoli Saheb, Goindwal.

The formation of the Khalsa was seen as a threat by the hill chiefs; hence they approached the emperor of Delhi who ordered the governors of Sirhind and Lahore to march against the Guru. They started attacking Anandpur and continued these attacks for three years – exhausting the resources of the Guru. He moved to Sirsa, where yet again, a battle was fought. The Guru was separated from his family. His mother Mata Gujari, and his two sons, Zoravar Singh and Fateh Singh, took shelter with an old servant. The old servant betrayed them and handed them over to Wazir Khan, the governor of Sirhind. Wazir Khan cruelly put the children to death, in spite of the protests of the Nawab of Malerkotla. Mata Gujari – their grandmother – could not survive the shock of their death and breathed her last. The Guru was followed to Chamkaur, where he was besieged along with his band of 40 Sikhs. Two of his sons died there in 1705 – facing the enemy stoically.

The Guru disguised himself as *Ucch ka Pir*, or a revered Muslim saint, and escaped from the enemy soldiers. He moved to Jatpura, where he was befriended by Rai Kalha who offered his allegiance to the Guru. When the Guru came to know about his two sons who had been killed in Sirhind, he took leave of Rai Kalha and built another army for the last battle. The battle that followed at Muktsar between the royal forces and the Sikhs was one of the bloodiest ever fought, and the Sikhs emerged victorious.

After a lot of struggle, the Guru reached Talvandi Sabo, now called Damdama, in 1706 and stayed here for nine months with an influential Sikh called Dalla. The place is known as Guru ki Kashi. It was here that the Guru recited the whole Adi Granth (Guru Granth Sahib) and added the verses of the ninth master, Guru Tegh Bahadur. The place is marked by the Takhat Damdama Sahib. On the way, when Guru Gobind Singh was at Dina, he sent a letter in Persian verse in reply to the summons from Aurangzeb. He called it *Zafarnama*, an epistle of victory.

When he reached the neighbourhood of Baghor in Rajputana, he heard the news of Aurangzeb's death in his camp at Ahmadnagar, sometime during the last week of February in 1707. Bahadur Shah, Aurangzeb's eldest son, rushed down from Peshawar to claim the throne. A battle with his brother Azam was fought on 8 June 1707 at Jajua, near Agra, that determined Bahadur Shah to be the new ruler. The Guru showed his support for Bahadur Shah, and after Bahadur Shah's victory, presented him with a rich dress of honour. He remained with Bahadur Shah, and marched into Rajputana against the Kachvahas, and thence to Deccan to suppress the insurrection of his brother Kam Bakhsh. There were two Pathans who were also following the Guru from Punjab, and at Nanded, after acquainting themselves with the Guru, attacked him with a fatal blow. On 7 October 1708, Guru Gobind breathed his last.

He had earlier chosen Banda Bairagi – later known as Banda Singh Bahadur. The Guru asked him to go to Panjab and lead the Sikhs. Before his final moment, Guru Gobind Singh proclaimed the Adi Granth to be the Guru – forever after – for the Sikhs.

TOP: *Marbles Guru Gobind Singh played with in his childhood at Patna.*
ABOVE: Chaki, *stone grinder of Mata Gujari, Patna.*

ABOVE: Dastar *(turban) of Guru Hargobind from the collection of Sangha family of Drolli Bhai Ki.*
LEFT: Seal of Guru Gobind Singh from the collection of Takhat Damdama Sahib.
FACING PAGE: A sword of Guru Gobind Singh from the collection of Dalla family near Takhat Damdama Sahib.

LEFT: Nagini Barcha *of Guru Gobind Singh at Takhat Keshgarh Sahib, Anandpur.*

FACING PAGE: Guru Gobind Singh's weapons (from left to right): 1. A forked and serrated khanda *with inscription in Gurmukhi –* 'Ek Onkar, Sat Guru Prasad, Degh Tegh Fateh, Nusrat Badrang, Yaft Az Nanak Guru Gobind Singh'; *2. A sword with gold hilt and hunting scenes inscribed on the blade; 3. Hilt of a sword with gold and pearl inlay; 4. A* katar *(punch dagger); 5. A sword given to Baba Rama and Taloka in 1696 engraved in Gurmukhi with words reading* 'Guru Gobind Singh Akal Sahai Degh Tegh Fateh Darshan Karega so Nihal'; *6. Kirpan with gold hilt. From the Collection of Maharaja of Patiala at Moti Bagh Palace.*

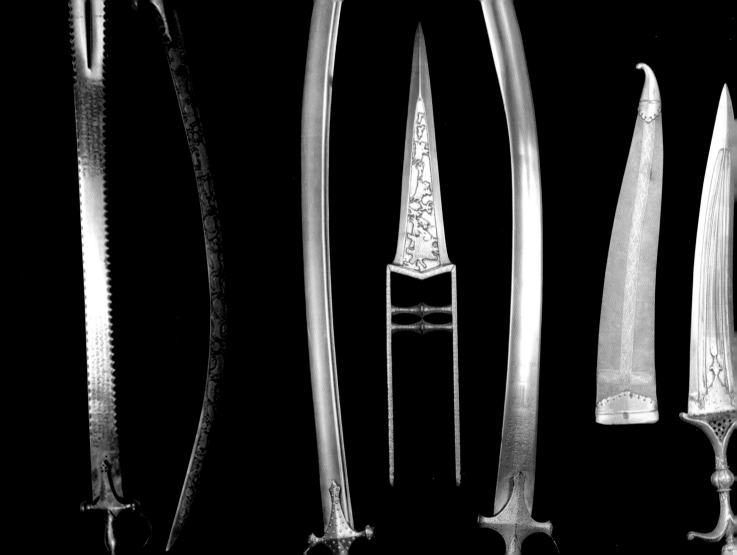

LEFT: *Maha Kali axe of Guru Gobind Singh.*
RIGHT: *Safajang, a battle axe presented by Guru Gobind Singh to Baba Rama and Taloka.*

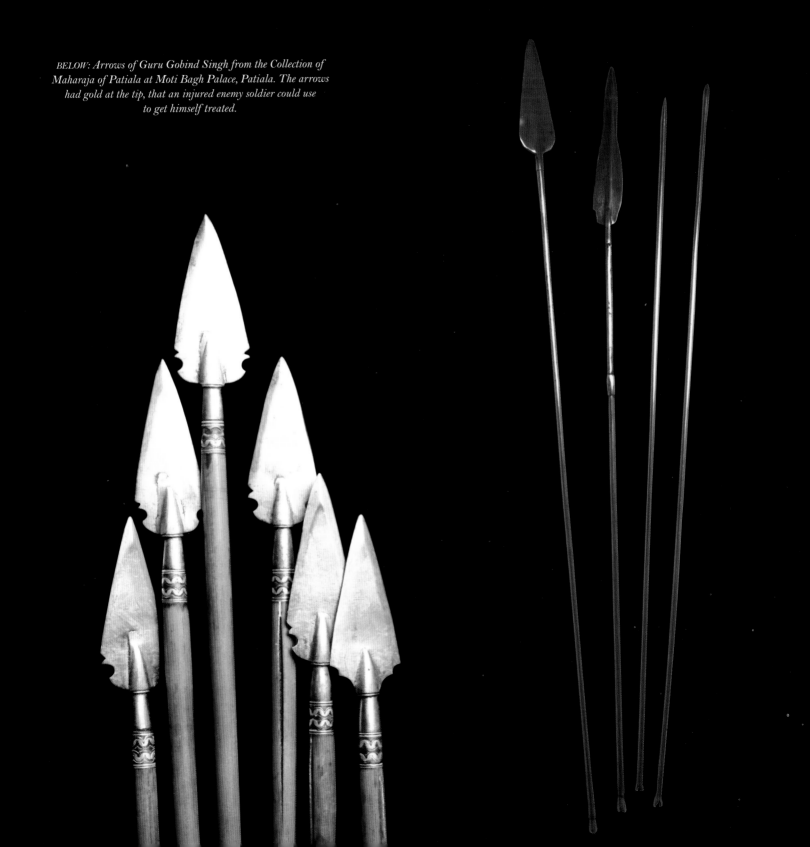

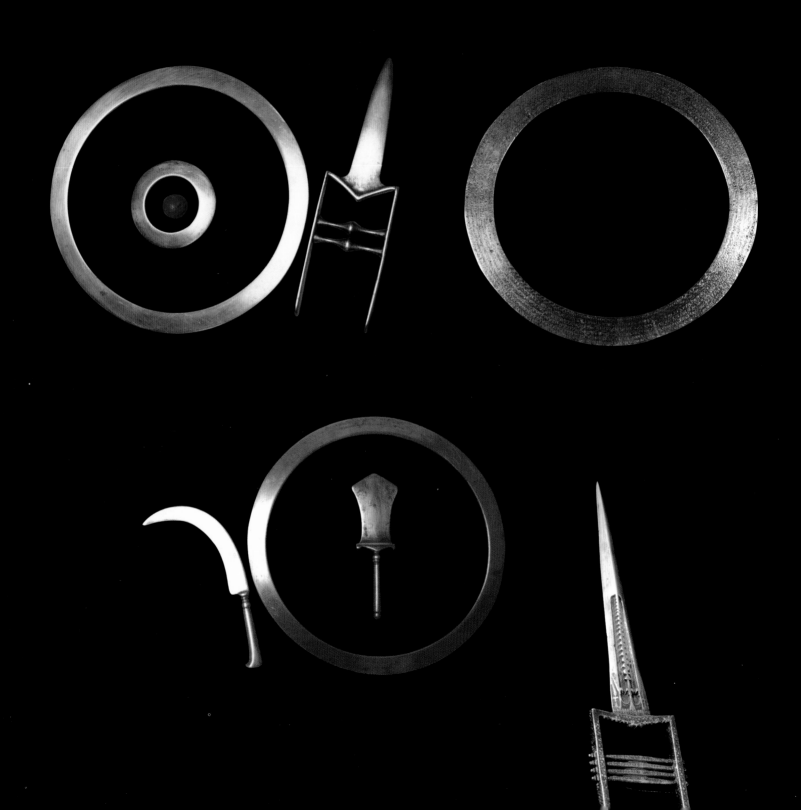

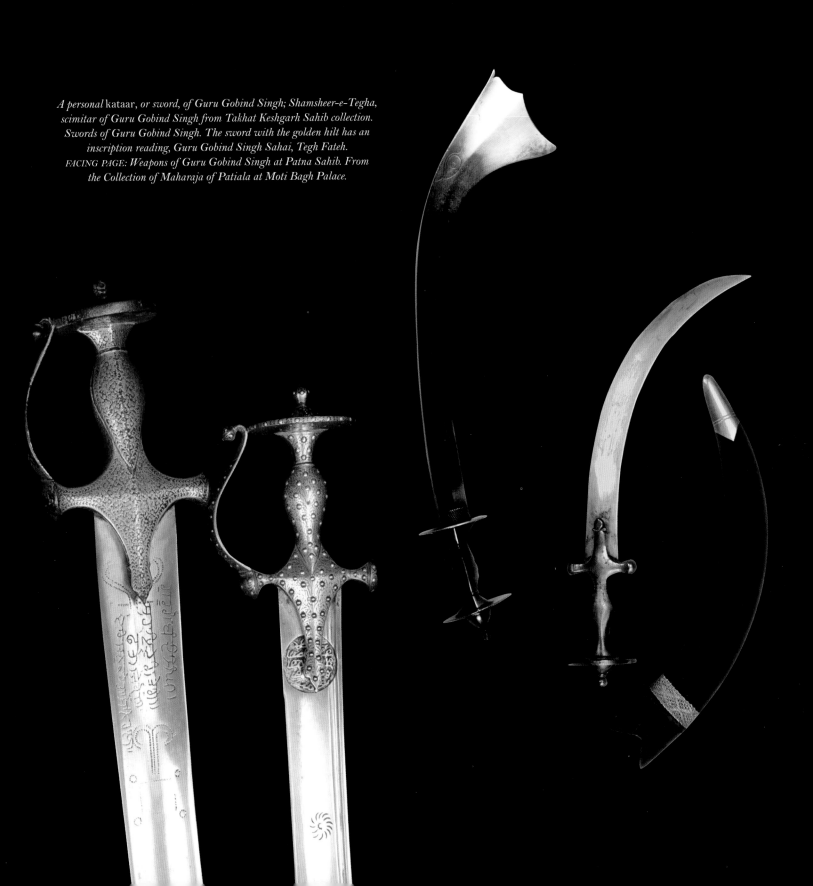

*A personal kataar, or sword, of Guru Gobind Singh; Shamsheer-e-Tegha,
scimitar of Guru Gobind Singh from Takhat Keshgarh Sahib collection.
Swords of Guru Gobind Singh. The sword with the golden hilt has an
inscription reading, Guru Gobind Singh Sahai, Tegh Fateh.
FACING PAGE: Weapons of Guru Gobind Singh at Patna Sahib. From
the Collection of Maharaja of Patiala at Moti Bagh Palace.*

ABOVE AND FACING PAGE: Gurdwara Hemkund Sahib is situated at a height of 15,000 feet above the sea level. The climb to the gurdwara begins from Gobind Ghat on the Badrinath highway in the state of Uttarakhand. In the Bachitra Natak, the Guru while mentioning about his previous birth says that he did intense meditation close to a lake surrounded by seven snow-clad peaks. With the efforts of Sohan Singh, Modan Singh and Bhai Vir Singh, the place was discovered and a small gurdwara was built in 1936. In the year 1937, Guru Granth Sahib was installed at the gurdwara. Also seen (above) are the Brahma Kamals, a rare flower, popularly known as the king of the Himalayan flowers.

90

A portrait of Guru Gobind Singh from the Collection of Maharaja of Patiala at Moti Bagh Palace.
RIGHT: Sikh devotees during Jor Mela at Gurdwara Fatehgarh Sahib in Sirhind. The mela, or fair, is organized in the memory of Sahibzada Fateh Singh and Sahibzada Zorawar Singh, two teenage sons of Guru Gobind Singh. The two were entombed while still alive on 26 December 1704 on the orders of the Governor of Sirhind, Wazir Khan.

CHAPTER II

HARMANDIR
The Abode of Tranquility

THE HARMANDIR OR DURBAR SAHIB, SITUATED IN AMRITSAR, HAS BEEN AN IMPORTANT CENTRE FOR THE SIKHS SINCE ITS INCEPTION. ITS SHEER PRESENCE, MAGNIFICENCE, AND HISTORICAL VALUE EMBODY THE THOUGHTS AND THE SOUL OF SIKH ARCHITECTURE. THE HARMANDIR WAS THE OUTCOME OF THE COLLECTIVE VISION OF THE SIKH GURUS WHO WERE GREAT TOWN PLANNERS AND BUILDERS. IT WAS GURU RAMDAS WHO DUG THE TANK, AND LAID THE FOUNDATION OF THE CITY OF AMRITSAR, THEN CALLED CHAK GURU RAMDAS, OR RAMDASPURA. WHEN ONE STEPS INTO THE *DEORHI* OF GOLDEN TEMPLE, ONE EXPERIENCES THE MAGNIFICENCE OF THE TEMPLE COMPLETELY ENGULFING AN INDIVIDUAL IN A SPIRITUAL AND DIVINE EXPERIENCE.

FACING PAGE: Har ki Pauri at Harmandir Sahib.

The city of Amritsar was built when Guru Ramdas began establishing a town close to the water body and invited traders from 52 different backgrounds to settle there. Many different markets were established in the town, known as *katras* – each specializing in a different business. Under the leadership of Guru Arjan, the construction of Harmandir was envisaged. He invited the great Muslim Sufi saint of Lahore, Hazrat Mian Mir, to lay the foundation stone in December 1588. Guru Arjan Dev designed the Harmandir in a manner that the main structure was constructed in the middle of the pool and has entrances in all four directions signifying that all are welcome here. Sitting under the *lachi ber* tree near the Darshani Deorhi, the Guru supervised the construction of the building. The mobilization by the Guru for the construction work involved the Sikhs on a massive scale. The Sikhs poured in resources of all kinds in large volumes, perhaps making the *karseva* one of the biggest endeavours undertaken in its time. The Guru was assisted by Baba Budha and Bhai Gurdas. The temple was completed in 1604. Guru Arjan Dev installed the holy book in it, and appointed Baba Budha Ji as the first granthi of the Harmandir Sahib in 1604.

It is believed that the Granth, wrapped in silk *rumalas*, was brought to the sanctum sanctorum in a palanquin. The Granth was placed on the cot and Baba Budha, who was in charge of the proceedings, was asked to open the Granth and read out a hymn to the devotees. Thus began the tradition of listening to the kirtan from the Granth that has remained unbroken ever since. It also was indicative of the times when the words from the Granth were to guide the Sikh community the world over.

The tradition of kirtan has prevailed since the times of Guru Arjan. There have also been sometime adjustments with regard to winter and summer timings. After the palanquin, also known as the Palki sahib carrying the Guru Granth Sahib is taken to the Akal Takhat, the sanctum sanctorum is taken over by devout Sikhs, who – under the guidance of *sevadars* – clean everything with milk while continuously reciting Gurbani. The *kiwad*, or the portals, open as early as 2:15 am depending on the time of the year. From mid-October until mid-February, the *kiwads* open at 3:00 am. As soon as the *kiwads* open, the melodious kirtan begins. Between 3:30 am and 4:00 am, depending on the time of the year, the kirtan of *Asa Di War* begins. From 4:30 am to 5:15 am, the departure of Palki sahib takes place from the Akal Takhat amidst the sound of *narsingha*, an instrument that is symbolic of the movement of royal entourage. The Guru Granth Sahib is installed on the Peera Sahib, a small cot, amidst *simran* by devout Sikhs. Throughout the day, kirtan is recited by various *ragi jathas* and nowadays, with the advancement of technology, kirtan can also be heard on radio, television and other electronic devices. In the afternoon, Anand Sahib is recited, followed by Charan Kamal Aarti, at 3:00 pm. From 5:00 pm to 6:15 pm the *ragi jathas* recite *Sodar*, and from 6:45 pm to 8:00 pm they perform *aarti*. After the evening *ardaas*, kirtan resumes and goes on up to 9:45 pm until the last *hukamnama*. At 10:00 pm, Guru Granth Sahib is taken in the palki sahib back to the Akal Takhat and Sukhasan is performed.

The architecture of Harmandir Sahib is the foundation of Sikh architecture. It was influenced by the architectural styles prevalent at the time in which it was built, but the Guru brought forward a distinct Sikh symbology. The architecture of Harmandir moves away from the traditional Hindu style of temple architecture by building it at a lower level as opposed to a raised platform. The worshippers had to go down the steps in order to enter it. The main structure of Harmandir is built on a 67-feet-wide square platform in the centre of the tank and the temple itself is a 40 feet square. It has a door in each direction, and the Darshani Deorhi stands at the shore end of the causeway. The bridge that leads to the main building is 202 feet in length and 21 feet in width. The door of Darshani Deorhi is 10 feet in height and 8 feet 6 inches in width. The archway on the western side of the pool opens on to the causeway bordered with balustrades of fretted marble with lamps set upon marble columns. The main structure leads to *Har ki Pauri*. The structure of the Harmandir Sahib has three floors, and on each floor is the Prakash of Guru Granth Sahib. At the top, a 4 feet high parapet rises on all the sides. It has four attics on its four corners, and above the central hall of the main sanctuary is the third storey that has a small square room. On the top of this room is a low fluted dome bearing a lotus motif at the base, and an inverted lotus above it that is supporting the *Kalash*. It has a beautiful *chattri* at the top. The artisans came from all walks of life, and hence there are various influences that blend and can be noticed around the complex.

The structure, constructed by Guru Ramdas, was levelled to the ground during the attacks by Ahmad Shah Abdali's general, Jahan Khan. However, in response, a Sikh Army, sent to hunt down the Afghan force, was under strict orders to show no mercy. The Sikhs were decisively victorious in the ensuing battle. Both forces met five miles outside Amritsar where Jahan Khan's army was destroyed. He himself was decapitated by the commander Sardar Dayal Singh. As soon as Afghans left Punjab, the Sikhs reconstructed it. By the latter half of the eighteenth century, Sikhs had gradually begun to be influential in the political scenario of Punjab.

The beautification of the Harmandir or the Golden Temple – as we now know it – dates back to the early nineteenth century. It was led by Maharaja Ranjit Singh, who decided to adorn the structure with gold. At his invitation, the best artisans and craftsmen poured into Amritsar on a large scale. The Maharaja considered it his pristine privilege to serve the Harmandir by being instrumental in its gold plating. He donated Rs 5,00,000 for the gold work on the roof, and the task was executed by Mistri Yar Mohammad Khan, under the supervision of Bhai Sand Singh. Many Sikh leaders came forward to donate for the gold plating, for instance Tara Singh Gheba, Pratap Singh, Jodh Singh, and Ganda Singh Peshawari.

There are some 300 fascinating patterns on the structures. The murals inside the building have floral patterns that are interspersed with animal motifs. The murals depicting human figures that are seen on the front side, for instance, are two embossed copper panels, the lower representing Guru Nanak flanked by Bala and Mardana, and the upper on the wall, behind the stairway leading to the top of the shrine, represents Guru Gobind Singh on a horseback. The doors of the Darshani Deorhi, which is the entrance to the Harmandir, depict beautiful ivory inlay work. The door is made of *shisham* overlaid with silver, and the back of the door is inlaid with ivory. The gold for the Darshani Deorhi was donated by Sangat Singh, the raja of the state of Jind. The Darshani Deorhi Arch stands at the mouth of the causeway to the Harmandir Sahib; it is 202 feet (62 m) high and 21 feet (6 m) wide. The lower parts of the sanctum sanctorum are of beautiful, soft marble and the upper portion is covered with gilded gold. At the very centre, the Guru Granth Sahib is placed under a stunning canopy studded with jewels. The floral patterns that strike visitors as soon as they step in, is the work of Muslim artisans from Chiniot, now in Pakistan. On the second floor is the beautiful and dazzling Sheesh Mahal – a room full of mirrors! The work seen on this floor is known as Gach. It is intricate work inlaid with coloured glass. The inlaying of coloured cut-stones in marble, found on the lower portions of the exterior walls of the shrine, is known as *jaratkari* work. In fact, the work is *pâte dure* and the inlay comprises semi-precious stones, such as lapis lazuli and onyx. Here, one finds many devoted men and women submerged in the divine ambience surroundings offer. Following the small stretch of stairs on the corner takes one to a square pavilion on the top floor, which is surmounted by a low fluted dome, lined at the base with a number of smaller domes. There are four kiosks at the corner. The site of Akal Takhat through the domes is beautiful. This combination of the domes along with the views of the majestic *sarovar*, *sangat*, and the parikrama create a serene ambience.

Inside the temple complex, there are many shrines of the past Sikh gurus, saints, and martyrs. There are three jujube trees (*ber*), each signifying a historical event. *Ath Sath Tirath*, which is past the *Dukh Bhanjani Ber*, is a raised platform from where Guru Arjan supervised the construction of the temple. *Dukh Bhanjani Ber* is associated with Rajni, the daughter of Duni Chand Khatri of the Patti village. One day, when Duni Chand asked his five daughters who it was that provided them with everything? – All his daughters replied that he did, except Rajni, who said it was God. Rajni's utterance provoked her father who got her married to a leper as punishment. She heard about Guru Ramdas constructing a new city at Amritsar, and decided to move there along with her husband. Every day, she made arrangements for her husband under the *ber* tree and went to help the *sangat* in the kitchen. Her husband witnessed a strange incident, he noticed that black crows took a dip in the water and came out white. This made him realize that this was no ordinary pool of water. He pushed himself close to the water and took a dip, only to find that he had been fully cured. Since then, the *ber* tree is known as *Dukh Bhanjani Ber*.

Another tree, the *Lachi Ber*, is situated in the precincts of the complex, from where Baba Budha supervised the construction of the Harmandir. It is important to note that these trees have been witnesses to the unfolding of the Sikh history. They have given shade to many devotees who came to Sri Harmandir. Baba Deep Singh, a brave martyr breathed his last in the parikrama where now stands Gurdwara Baba Deep Singh Shaheed.

Gurdwara Manji Sahib is where Guru Arjan Dev would sit on a *manji* (cot) after a day's work and discuss matters with *sevadars*.

The nine-storey, and 108-feet high is the Gurdwara of Baba Atal, son of Guru Hargobind, a spiritually gifted boy who died at the age of nine.

Gurdwara Thara Sahib, associated with Guru Tegh Bahadur, is a *thara* (platform) with twelve sides. The main entrance is on its east side and a baradari adorns its apex. The site marks the spot where Guru Tegh Bahadur came to pay his respects, but the complex was under the control of Sodhi Harji, the grandson of Prithi Chand, who did not permit the Guru to enter the complex. On refusal, the Guru rested at the *thara*, where this shrine now stands.

Gurdwara Mata Kaulan, also famous as Kaulsar Sahib is situated on the west side of the Baba Atal Gurdwara. Mata Kaulan was a Muslim spiritual lady who was the adopted daughter of the Qazi of Lahore, and because of the atrocities of the Qazi, took refuge with Guru Hargobind, at Amritsar. She was brought by Mian Mir to the Guru. The work on the Kaulsar was executed by Baba Budha ji, the first head of the Golden Temple. The samadh of Mata Kaulan is located at the end of Kaulsar Gurdwara.

THE MANAGEMENT

From the very beginning, the Harmandir Sahib was envisaged by the Gurus to have a special place for the Sikhs. This was clearly reflected in action when Bhai Gurdas and Baba Budha were asked to manage the affairs of the place by Guru Arjan. After the execution of Guru Arjan, Guru Hargobind shifted his base from Amritsar to Kiratpur, and the control of the Gurdwara was taken over by the *masands*, who were faithful to Sodhi Meharban, the son of Prithi Chand. Prithi Chand was the elder brother of Guru Arjan who was not given the Sikh Guruship. His son Sodhi

Harji converted the Harmandir into his personal property for five decades. The absolute control of the *masands* can be understood from the fact that when Guru Tegh Bahadur visited Harmandir, he was denied entry into the premises. From here, the Guru went to Anandpur Sahib.

After Sodhi Harji died, his sons could not maintain the control over the shrine. Guru Gobind Singh, after the formation of the Khalsa in the year 1699, sent Bhai Mani Singh to take charge of the management of the temple and to carry out much needed improvements. He instructed the Sikhs through *hukamnamas* to assist him. The Sikhs were unable to get much done due to the political turmoil that engulfed them since the death of Guru Gobind Singh in 1708. The control of the Harmandir was taken over by the *Udasi* sect.

The affairs of the Harmandir were in a state of dismay, Mata Sundari, at the time stationed in Delhi, deputed Bhai Mani Singh along with Bhai Kirpal Singh to take control of the shrine. Bhai Mani Singh took charge as the granthi of the Harmandir and became the Jathedar of Akal Bunga. He organized the management of Harmandir. The Sikhs began organizing themselves as *dals*, and started looting government revenue. Harmandir remained prominent rallying point for the centre, rather, it appears that the Sikhs began considering it their centre. The Sikh groups decided to assemble on the occasions of Diwali and Baisakhi festivals. Bhai Mani Singh sought permission to celebrate Diwali in Harmandir Sahib. It was granted subject to a fees of Rs 5,000. Bhai Mani Singh sent invitations to the Sikhs to visit the temple, however, the Mughal forces discouraged the Sikhs from celebrating at the shrine. Bhai Mani Singh was unable to pay the fees and he was asked to either choose Islam or to die. His body was cut limb for limb.

In the following years, when Nadir Shah was on his journey from Delhi, the Sikhs looted his entourage. He asked Zakariya Khan about the men who looted his booty, to which Zakariya Khan replied that these men are group of fakirs who visit their holy tank twice a year, bathe, and then disappear. Nadir Shah promptly remarked that the day is not far when these rebels will take possession of the country.

The Harmandir was taken over by the Lahore government in 1740. Massa Rangar, a local zamindar even converted the shrine into a stable and the inner most sanctuary into a nautch girl house. This was not acceptable to the people, and two Sikhs, Mehtab Singh and Sukha Singh of Mari Kambo reached Harmandir and beheaded Massa Rangar. The Lahore government intensified their movement to kill the Sikhs. The Sikhs took risks and visited the Harmandir to take dip in the holy tank. The two dominant groups of the Sikhs – Budha Dal (group of Sikh elders) and Taruna Dal (group of young Sikhs), began meeting regularly at the Harmandir Sahib to organize the community. After the death of Zakariya Khan, the governor of Lahore, the *gurmatta* (decision arrived with consensus by the Sikh congregation) was passed to organize the Sikhs into *misls*.

Diwan Lakhpat Rai ordered the Harmandir to be desecrated and the tank was filled with earth. Further, the Sikhs were brutally massacred in large numbers in 1746, the unfortunate incident is remembered as the Chota Ghalughara. A group of armed soldiers were deputed to shoot any Sikh who would try to take dip in the holy tank, but many Sikhs disguised in Turkish uniforms, and went ahead to pay their obeisance. On 30 March 1747, after a *gurmatta* passed by the Sikhs – a small fort called Ram Rauni, capable of accommodating 500 men, was built with watch towers and moat around it.

The Sikhs were beginning to gain sympathizers, such as Diwan Kaura Mal, who worked for Muin ul Mulk, the governor of Lahore. It was due to his efforts that the Sikhs got revenue for twelve villages and regained Ram Rauni. He also offered rupees 11,000 to the Harmandir Sahib. This conciliatory policy of Muin ul Mulk did not sustain, and soon he reverted to repressing the Sikhs. This did not last for very long as after his death, the Sikhs again flocked to the Harmandir in large numbers. This peace was disrupted with the Afghans taking over the control of the city in 1757. Under Jahan Khan, the Harmandir was demolished and its tank was filled with mud. The control of Harmandir Sahib was regained by the Sikhs when 500 khalsa soldiers, led by Baba Deep Singh, attacked the occupants of the shrine. In 1762, Ahmad Shah Durrani attacked the Sikhs during the Baisakhi festivities in Harmandir to establish his control over the region of Amritsar. The Sikhs retaliated in large numbers and pushed the army of Ahmad Shah Durrani back to Lahore. They cleaned the holy tank and took control for a brief period, before again getting embroiled with the Afghan forces. In 1765, the Sikhs had expanded their control on the region so much so that their power could not be ignored by the Afghans. Even more, the Afghans realized the importance of Harmandir for the Sikhs and did not attack the shrine again. The Sikhs, rallying around the Harmandir, were steadily becoming the masters of Punjab.

Harmandir's management was under the control of the Sikhs for a long period of time since the latter half of the eighteenth century. Maharaja Ranjit Singh paid respects to the Harmandir soon after he took over the city of Amritsar. He immediately granted jagirs to the granthis and other staff. In 1821, he spent Rs. 7 lakh for building gates and walls around the city. Earlier, many buildings were constructed by the *misl* chiefs. Under the instructions of the Bhangi chiefs, Mahants Pritam Das and Santokh Das got the Hansli canal constructed to carry water to the Harmandir. Maharaja Ranjit Singh took steps to embellish the shrine by offering gold plates for the dome, gates and walls of the temple.

The British took over Punjab in 1849, and tried to gain control of the administration of the Harmandir Sahib. Lehna Singh Majithia, Sardar Jodh Singh, Sardar Parduman Singh, and Bhai Makhan Singh assisted the British. Lehna Singh Majithia advised to appoint Sardar Jodh Singh as the in-charge. In 1859, Jodh Singh was appointed the Surbrah of the temple. He heard all the disputes, had power to expel any priest and also to distribute temple income. He kept himself updated on the happenings in the shrine and its vicinity. No meeting could be held without his permission. He was presented *khillat* (a ceremonial gift) by the British for his excellent services rendered. The management of the Harmandir remained under the watchful eyes of the British until it was handed over to Shiromani Gurdwara Prabandhak Committee (SGPC) in 1925.

JALAO: EPITOME OF DEVOTION TOWARDS HARMANDIR

The Harmandir Sahib has touched the hearts and souls of many people. To demonstrate their gratitude towards their Guru, many Sikhs offered priceless gifts to the temple. These gifts are brought out of the *toshakhana*, the treasury of the Harmandir, on six events every year. These occasions are the birth days of Guru Nanak, Guru Ramdas, Guru Tegh Bahadur, Guru Gobind Singh, Guru Hargobind Sahib, Gurgaddi Diwas, and the first Prakash of Sri Guru Granth Sahib. The articles of *jalao* are taken to allocated places in Harmandir, Akal Takhat, and Baba Atal for display. After the display, the articles are redeposited in the *toshakhana*. The treasury is opened by the manager of Durbar Sahib, head granthi, and the nominated members.

Maharaja Ranjit Singh presented to Harmandir a canopy made of gold, weighing twenty pounds and studded with emeralds, diamonds, rubies, and pearls. Also, on seeing a beautifully crafted *sehra*, prepared for his grandson – Nau Nihal Singh, he ordered it to be given to the Harmandir. Some of the other relics displayed during the *jalao* are: the four gold gates, gold chattris, golden frills, gold hand fans, the golden sword of Maharaja Ranjit Singh, and fly whisk made from sandalwood presented by a Muslim saint. These articles are kept with care in their respective castings, cushions and wrappers under lock and key. The *toshakhana* is always guarded.

KARSEVA: LABOUR OF LOVE

The ideals of altruistic contribution and community service were important thoughts behind the Sikh ethos – right from the very beginning. Guru Arjan himself performed *karseva* with fellow Sikhs from all over the Indian subcontinent. In 1746, when Ahmad Shah Abdali ordered the ransacking of the shrine, the Sikhs rebuilt the Harmandir by performing *karvseva*. Yet again, the temple was destroyed in 1757 by Jahandar Khan. The Sikhs, in large numbers performed *karseva* in 1758. In 1842, another *karseva* was performed under the leadership of Bhai Gurmukh Singh Giani.

One more historic *karseva* was performed in the year 1923 during the Gurdwara Reform Movement. The *seva* of the holy tank was started on 17 June by the Panj Piaras, who did so by lifting the sledge with gold spades and silver pans after offering prayers with the Maharaja of Patiala and other Sikh chiefs. These precious gold and silver tools are kept in the *toshakhana*.

In recent times, *karseva* was performed in 1985 to cleanse the holy tank after Operation Blue Star. In 1986, as decided by the Sarbat Khalsa, the Sikhs decided to rebuild the Akal Takhat – the seat of the timeless one. It took nine years to build the new and more spacious structure. The *karseva* is not unique to the Sikh community, but the manner in which every Sikh looks forward to being a part of it is unique to the divine energy that binds Sikhs the world over. This is when the hands of the rich and poor come together in the labour of love for their Guru's home.

The Harmandir Sahib has been instrumental in providing both, a clear spiritual paradigm and also a platform from where many Sikh movements were launched. It has been a factor that has united the Sikhs whenever tyranny has become the rule of the day in Punjab. It is the venue of Sarbat Khalsa, a process by which the Sikhs get together and take significant decisions for the benefit of the community. During earlier times, in any moment of need, the Sikh *misls* used to come together to address vital matters and further the cause of the community. One of the major mass movements that had its origin at the Harmandir was the Gurdwara Reform Movement of 1920–25. In independent India, the Punjabi Suba movement, which demanded a Punjabi-speaking state was initiated from this holy place. More recently, the Harmandir was the venue of the act of Operation Blue Star that led to the demolition of the Akal Takhat.

For centuries to come, Harmandir Sahib will continue to unite, bind, and be the nucleus for Sikhs worldwide.

A group of women doing sewa *of washing utensils. Many visitors to the Harmandir Sahib take out time and do* sewa, *or selfless service that is one of the important pillars of Sikhism.*
FACING PAGE: A 60-metre causeway connects Sri Harmandir Sahib to the entrance, the Darshani Deorhi. The Harmandir Sahib is surrounded by a sarovar, amrit sar, or pool of nectar, and this is the only way to reach the sanctum sanctorum. There are long queues of devotees, who slowly make their way into the gurdwara.

Sangat *paying respects at Nishaan Sahib (Flagpoles) at the Akal Takhat Sahib. The Nishan Sahib in the Sikh tradition means the 'holy flag' or 'exalted ensign' – symbolic of the values of the Sikh faith. The Nishan Sahibs in front of the* takhat *are indicative of two swords,* miri *and* piri, *of Guru Hargobind, thus signifying the temporal and spiritual values instilled in the Sikh faith by the Guru.*
FACING PAGE: *Dargah of Sufi Muslim Saint Mian Mir, who laid the foundation stone of Sri Harmandir Sahib, is situated in Lahore, Pakistan. Mian Mir was invited by Guru Arjan to lay the foundation stone of the Sri Harmandir Sahib.*
It was laid on 13 January 1588 AD.

The sanctum sanctorum of Harmandir Sahib, Amritsar.
FACING PAGE: *After the evening* paath *(service), the holy book is taken in a ceremonial procession to*
Kotha Sahib, or the resting place. The holy book is carried back to the sanctum sanctorum of
Harmandir Sahib at the divine hour of dawn in a golden palanquin.

ABOVE: Interior of Harmandir Sahib is lavishly decorated with inlay marble work, along with painted and gilded designs.
RIGHT: Inside the sanctum sanctorum, passages are read from the Guru Granth Sahib throughout the day.

The sanctum's ceiling is gilded, embossed and decorated with mirror-work. The walls inside are richly embellished with floral patterns. The frescoes follow the Indian traditional nature motifs. The rare art work is an example of the finest craftsmanship of the artists. At the top is again a small pavilion that is surmounted by a fluted golden dome, lined with small ones at its base. There are four chattris, or kiosks, at the corners, and with the small domes around they create a beautiful reflection in the sarovar.

ABOVE AND FOLLOWING PAGES 110-111: Rarely shown to the public, gold panels depicting scenes from the lives of the Sikh Gurus on the doors of Harmandir Sahib were presented by Maharaja Ranjit Singh. These doors are displayed during Jalao ceremony, when special articles from the toshakhana of the Sri Harmandir Sahib, are shown to the public.

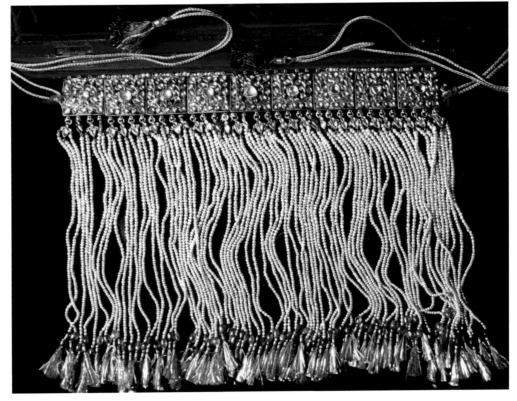

RIGHT, ABOVE: Priceless gifts presented by Maharaja Ranjit Singh and other Sikh chiefs stored in the toshakhana *(treasury) of the Harmandir Sahib, which are displayed only on special occasions.*

RIGHT, BELOW: Wedding sehra of Nau Nihal Singh, grandson of Maharaja Ranjit Singh preserved in the toshakhana *of the Harmandir Sahib.*

FACING PAGE, FAR LEFT: A peacock made of sapphire and studded with diamonds, rubies and pearls was presented by Maharaja Ranjit Singh and preserved in the toshakhana *of the Golden Temple.*

RIGHT: Priceless gifts stored in toshakhana *are displayed during 'jalao' ceremony on four occasions inside the Harmandir Sahib.*

113

114

ABOVE AND RIGHT: *Next to Dukh Bhanjani Beri is the place known as Ath Sath Tirath, which signifies that anyone taking a dip here with devotion will have the benefit of visiting 68 holy places. Devotees spend time on this raised marble platform and recite small* gutkas *(manuscripts) of Gurbani.*

116

Coinciding with Diwali, the festival of lights is celebrated as Bandi Chhor Diwas, or Day of Liberation by the Sikhs. On this day, the sixth Sikh Guru, Guru Hargobind, returned to Amritsar in 1619, after being released (along with 52 princes) from the Gwalior prison by the Mughal Emperor Jahangir. There are fireworks at Harmandir Sahib to mark the festival.

CHAPTER III

TEMPORAL SEATS
The Five Takhats

GURU HARGOBIND BUILT THE AKAL TAKHAT FACING THE HARMANDIR SAHIB, AND THUS BEGAN A NEW ERA IN SIKHISM. THE *TAKHAT* BECAME A CONVERGING POINT FOR PEOPLE FROM ALL WALKS OF LIFE — FROM THE COMMON MAN TO ELITE, FROM A BANKER TO A LENDER, FROM A FARMER TO A TRADER, FROM A SCHOLAR TO AN ILLITERATE — WHO CAME TO SEEK ADVICE, SHARE THEIR GRIEVANCES AND GET CLARIFICATIONS ABOUT THEIR FAITH. WHAT MAY HAVE APPEARED TO HAVE BEEN A SIMPLE BRICK-LAID PLATFORM BECAME THE SEAT OF THE TEMPORAL AUTHORITY FOR THE SIKHS. WHILE THE SIKHS SOUGHT ANSWERS AND DIRECTIONS TO THEIR INNER BEING FROM THE HARMANDIR, THEY COULD SEEK ANSWERS WITH REGARDS TO THE OUTER WORLD FROM THE INSTITUTION OF THE *TAKHAT*. FROM HERE, THE SIKHS RECEIVED *HUKAMNAMAS*, MEANING ORDERS, FROM THE GURU. THROUGH THESE *HUKAMNAMAS*, SIKHS HAVE BEEN PROVIDED WITH GUIDANCE AND CLARIFICATION ON DOCTRINES AND TRADITION. THESE *HUKAMNAMAS* ARE APPLICABLE TO ALL SIKHS THE WORLD OVER. AS SIKH HISTORY PROGRESSED, FOUR OTHER *TAKHATS*, NAMELY TAKHAT SRI DAMDAMA SAHIB, TAKHAT SRI HAZUR SAHIB, TAKHAT SRI KESHGARH SAHIB, AND TAKHAT SRI PATNA SAHIB WERE CHOSEN BY THE SIKH COMMUNITY TO BE THE ASSOCIATED TEMPORAL SEATS. ALL THE *TAKHATS* ARE ASSOCIATED WITH GURU GOBIND SINGH.

FACING PAGE: A sevadar *beats a drum at Takhat Keshgarh Sahib.*

*Built by Guru Hargobind, the sixth Guru, the Akal Takhat, the eternal
throne, is one of five* takhats *(seats of temporal power) of the Sikhs. It is
located in the Harmandir Sahib complex, facing the sanctum sanctorum
at an angle. While the Harmandir represents spiritual power, the Akal
Takhat represents temporal power. It is a place of justice and consideration
of temporal issues that face the Sikh community. It is from here that
Hukamnamas (resolutions) are announced providing guidance or
clarification on any point of Sikh doctrine or practice.*

121

SRI AKAL TAKHAT SAHIB

The Akal Takhat, or the Everlasting Throne – is the supreme seat of religious and temporal authority for the Sikhs. It stands in the confines of the Durbar Sahib complex facing the Harmandir and is the institution towards which every Sikh looks for guidance, clarification and inspiration. Since its inception, the *takhat* has played a role both as a venue and as an instrument in deciding upon the socio-religious and the political fate of the Sikhs, especially through the institutions of *gurmattas* and *hukamnamas*. It is the symbolic epitome of the continued tradition of *miri-piri* instilled by the sixth master – Guru Hargobind – which values the fact that righteousness must be defended with a rosary in one hand and a sword in the other.

Upholding the spirit of religious freedom, Guru Arjan Dev refused to convert to Islam. The Mughal authority took it as a disgrace and ordered the Guru to be tortured in the most inhuman manner. The Guru did not succumb to the physical and mental pressures and sacrificed himself for righteousness on 30 May 1606. Guru Hargobind (1595–1644), the son and successor of Guru Arjan Dev, changed his manner from the minimalism adopted by the earlier Gurus to magnificence, thus introducing new components into the community. He began wearing two swords – one symbolizing *Piri*, spiritualism and the other *Miri*, temporality. Opposite the Harmandir, he constructed the Akal Takhat to conduct the affairs of the Sikhs. He, along with Bhai Budha and Bhai Gurdas, completed its construction in the year 1606 with his own hands.

The Akal Takhat became central to the activities of the Sikhs. Bhai Gurdas, the principle caretaker of the Akal Takhat, issued *hukamnamas* to the Sikh *sangat* asking them to bring him the offering of horses and weapons. The Sikhs came to the meet Guru at the *takhat* and shared their concerns with him. Later, in 1635, Guru Hargobind shifted his base to Kiratpur and he left the control of the Harmandir in the hands of Guru Arjan Dev's elder brother Prithi Chand's son – Meharban. Subsequently, Hariji – Meharban's son – remained in charge of the Harmandir for nearly five decades.

It was after the creation of Khalsa in the year 1699 that Guru Gobind Singh sent Bhai Mani Singh to take charge of the Harmandir and the Akal Takhat. Subsequently, it was here that the Sikh groups got together during the festivities of Baisakhi and Diwali. This is where the Sikhs held *Sarbat Khalsa*, the massive gathering of the Sikhs to discuss the major issues affecting them. During the *Sarbat Khalsa* in 1745, the Sikhs organized themselves into twenty-five *jathas* or groups and later, in 1748, these groups formed the Dal Khalsa. The *takhat*, since its inception, has acted as the central stage in mobilizing the community. Even after Guru Gobind Singh, the *hukamnamas* were passed to the Sikh community by the *takhat*. All the Sikhs – royalty or commoner, rich or poor – have been abiding by the decree of the *takhat*. Even when Maharaja Ranjit Singh was summoned by the *takhat*, he humbly accepted the penalty imposed by the then Jathedar, Akali Phula Singh.

Several times in history, the *takhat*'s facade has been destroyed. Ahmad Shah Durrani destroyed it in 1762. But at the earliest occasion, the Sikhs held a *Sarbat Khalsa* in 1765 and rebuilt the *takhat*. The Sikh *sangat* built the first floor in 1774, and the remaining five storeys were built by Maharaja Ranjit Singh. The gilded dome of the *takhat* was funded by Hari Singh Nalwa. The Akal Takhat also faced severe damage during the Operation Blue Star in June 1984. The building was constructed twice, once by the Government of India and later by the Sikh panth through *karseva*.

FACING PAGE: A Sikh sevadar at Akal Takhat displays historical weapons belonging to Sikh Gurus and leaders in a ceremony held every evening. These weapons are preserved at the Akal Takhat.

ABOVE: *Miniature* kirpans *at the Akal Takhat.*
LEFT: *Collection of weapons at the Akal Takhat.*

Historic weapons belonging to Guru Gobind Singh, Guru Hargobind, Baba Ajit Singh, Baba Jujhar Singh, Baba Budha Sahib, Baba Deep Singh and other Sikh generals are kept in the Akal Takhat. These historic weapons include Sri Sahibs, teghs, katars, *guns,* chakarrs, *shields, and* khandas. *FOLLOWING PAGE (128): Sri Takhat Harmandir Sahib, Patna Sahib.*

127

TAKHAT SRI PATNA SAHIB

This *takhat* is located in the city of Patna, Bihar. The city was visited by the first master Guru Nanak and the ninth master Guru Tegh Bahadur. It was here that Guru Gobind Rai was born. Being the birthplace of the tenth Guru, the city is one of the most venerated places in Sikhism. Even the city's railway station is known as Patna Sahib, named after the *takhat*. There are many shrines that mark the important events associated with the Gurus.

Gurdwara Pahila Bara Gai Ghat marks the place where Guru Nanak stayed during his visit to Patna. It was the house of Bhai Jaita, a converted Sikh, who dedicated his life and home to the Guru. His home came to be known as Bari Sangat. En route to Assam, Guru Tegh Bahadur also stayed here with his family.

TAKHAT SRI HARMANDIR SAHIB

The congested streets of the old Patna city open up to the beautiful complex of the *takhat*. This used to be the residence of Salas Rai, a jeweller by profession, who was dedicated to the Gurus. Guru Nanak stayed here for nearly three months and preached to the people of Patna. The place became famous as Choti Sangat and was run by Adhraka, who was a devout Sikh and an employee of Salas Rai. When Guru Tegh Bahadur reached Patna, he left his family here in the care of his brother-in-law, Kirpal Chand. It was here that on 22 December 1666, Gobind Rai was born. There is a Hukam-e-khas, sent by the ninth Guru that is addressed to the Sikhs to take care of his family.

During Maharaja Ranjit Singh's time, a new building was constructed to mark the spot where Gobind Rai used to spend his early days. Later in 1887, the Sikh rulers of Patiala, Jind, and Faridkot constructed an extension of the main building that is a five-storey structure. The inner sanctum sanctorum is where Gobind Rai was born. There are three *palkis* – canopied seats – in the sanctum. The one in the centre facing the hall bears the Guru Granth Sahib. There are a number of relics associated with Guru Tegh Bahadur and Gobind Rai, which are kept here and give a peep into the young Guru and his family's life.

In a narrow lane close to Takhat Sahib stands **Gurdwara Bal Lila Maini Sangat**. Raja Fateh Chand and his wife were devout Sikhs who always wished for a child. Rani – the queen, developed fondness for the young Gobind Rai, who often came to their house and sat in her lap like her own son. She loved to take care of Gobind Rai and his friends and affectionately cooked boiled salted gram for them. Even today, if one visits the place, boiled salted gram are offered as prasad. There is a jujube tree in the compound of the gurdwara that is believed to have sprouted from the twig planted by Gobind Rai. A wood carving on the old front door is dated 28 August 1668. Unlike the other gurdwaras in Patna, this one is managed by the Nirmala sect.

Another place, famously known as Kangan Ghat, is where the young Gobind Rai used to play. It is situated a short walk from Takhat Patna Sahib on the banks of River Ganges. **Gurdwara Sri Guru Gobind Singh Ghat** is situated here. This ghat marks the spot where the young Gobind threw his golden bangle into the Ganga, demonstrating complete detachment from the material world. This was also where Shiv Dutt, a Brahmin, meditated and once felt in his vision that the young Gobind was a blessed soul; throughout his life he treated the young boy as such.

Not very far from the Takhat Patna Sahib, on the outskirts of the old city, is situated **Gurdwara Guru Ka Bagh**. This gurdwara marks the place where Guru Tegh Bahadur met his four-year-old son – Gobind, on his return to the city from Assam. It was an orchard owned by the Nawabs Rahim Baksh and Karim Baksh. The dried stump of the tamarind tree where the father and son met still stands.

LEFT: *Jathedar of Patna Sahib showing Hukme-i-Khas to the* sangat. *This* hukamnama *was issued by Guru Teg Bahadur to the sangat of Patna for their help to the Guru's family on the birth of Gobind Rai.*
RIGHT: *Kharawans of Guru Gobind Singh.* FACING PAGE: *Chola of Guru Gobind Singh.*

ABOVE: Pangora, *a small cot belonging to Guru Gobind Rai.*
BELOW: A dhal *belonging to Guru Gobind Singh is preserved at Takhat Patna Sahib.*

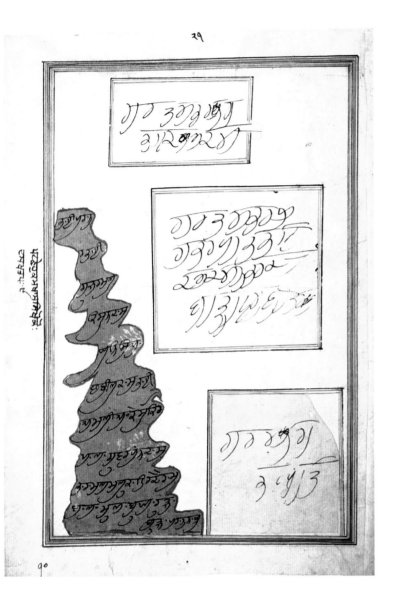

ABOVE: From a compendium of Hukamnamas *at Patna Sahib*

133

ਗੁਰੁ ਨਾਨਕਿ ਜੀਉ ॥੧॥

ABOVE AND FACING PAGE: Old paintings depicting Guru Nanak with Bhai Mardana playing rabab *at Patna Sahib.*
These folios are part of the compendium of Hukamnamas.

136

ABOVE AND FACING PAGE: From a compendium of Hukamnamas *at Patna Sahib showing calligraphy styles of Guru Teg Bahadur and Guru Gobind Singh. Birthplace of the tenth Guru, Guru Gobind Singh, the gurdwara at Patna Sahib was built by Maharaja Ranjit Singh in the eighteenth century.*

TAKHAT SRI KESHGARH SAHIB

Takhat Sri Keshgarh Sahib is situated on a hilltop at Anandpur Sahib, (literally 'The city of bliss') in Punjab. It is the one built at the exact place where the historic ceremony of the birth of the Khalsa panth took place on the day of Baisakhi, in 1699. The city was home to two Sikh Gurus, Guru Tegh Bahadur and Guru Gobind Singh, and for many years it witnessed history unfold.

The foundation of the city of Anandpur Sahib on the lower Shivalik hills was laid by Guru Tegh Bahadur in 1665. This land is the site of an old Makhowal village that was bought from the Rajput ruler of Kahlur (currently Bilaspur). The place was named Chak Nanaki, after the Guru's mother. From here, he travelled to various parts of the Indian subcontinent until 1672. The political scenario was changing rapidly and the Mughals began pursuing a proactive conversion policy. In 1675, a group of aggrieved Brahmins from Kashmir came to the Guru and begged to be saved from religious persecution and forcible conversion. They could only be saved by the intervention of a great soul. When the nine-year-old Gobind Rai noticed that his father was in deep thought about the plea of Kashmiri Brahmins, he immediately reacted, 'That soul could only be you'. The ninth Guru, on hearing this, resolved to go to the imperial capital, Delhi. He named his son Gobind Rai as his successor to the house of the Guru. He was taken into custody, and tortured to death at Chandni Chowk in Delhi on 11 November 1675. His body was taken by Lakhi Shah Banjara to the spot where Gurdwara Rakab Ganj stands today and cremated. The severed head was taken by Bhai Jaita to Anandpur Sahib, where Guru Gobind hugged Bhai Jaita and declared, '*Rangrete Guru Ke Bete*' (Rangretas are the sons of the Guru). Guru Gobind Singh cremated the head of Guru Tegh Bahadur at Anandpur Sahib, the place now marked as Sis Ganj Sahib. Gobind Rai, a child of nine, became the tenth Guru of the Sikhs here at Anandpur Sahib after the martyrdom of his father.

The young Gobind Rai wore weapons and asked the Sikhs to do the same in keeping the tradition of *Miri* and *Piri* alive. His actions, though peaceful, were considered to be threatening by the king of Kahlur, Bhim Chand. To avoid conflict, the Guru shifted his base to Sirmur at the invitation of its chief. It was there that he established Paonta Sahib, and lived till 1688. He returned to Chak Nanaki and renamed it Anandpur. He raised several forts – namely Keshgarh, Anandgarh, Lohgarh, Holgarh, Fatehgarh, and Taragarh. The forts were the site of many battles fought between the hill chiefs and the Sikhs, and each time the Sikhs were victorious.

Takhat Keshgarh marks the place where the new order of the Khalsa was revealed by Guru Gobind Singh on the day of Baisakhi in 1699. It was part of the Guru's vision to culminate the ideology of the prior nine Gurus into an everlasting pure force. He sent instructions to the Sikh sangat the world over, which urged them to not recognize the corrupt *masands*, and come over to Keshgarh on the decided time. A massive congregation of the Sikhs came together at the *takhat*. The Guru came out with a naked sword and asked for a head from his Sikhs. This was repeated five times until five Sikhs came forward. Each time the Guru took the Sikh inside a tent and came out with the sword in his hand dripping blood. Daya Ram – a Khatri, came from Lahore; Dharam Das – a Jat, from Hastinapur; Mohkam Chand – a washerman from Dwarka; Himmat – a watercarrier from Jagannath, and Sahib Chand – a barber, from Bidar, offered themselves to the Guru's call. The five Sikhs were then brought out wearing saffron coloured clothes and turbans. Each one of them carried a sword as well. All of them were initiated into the fold of the Khalsa as they imbibed the holy water, or *amrit*, which is a sweetened elixir mixed in a big utensil with *patashas*. The mixture was stirred with the aid of a

Khanda, a double edged sword. All the Panj Piaras – the five beloved khalsas – were asked to ordain *kangha* (comb), *kachchha* (pair of shorts), *kara* (steel bracelet), *kirpan* (sword), and *Kesh* (long hair). The Khalsa, shunning the caste system, asked the Sikh boys to use Singh and the Sikh women to use Kaur as their last name. After the five were initiated, the Guru bowed before them and asked them to initiate him to become a part of the new order. It is believed that thousands were initiated that day at Sri Anandpur Sahib.

The large gathering of Sikhs on the occasion of the birth of Khalsa made the hill chiefs insecure, and they attacked Anandpur. The Mughals supported the hill chiefs, and the emperor instructed his men to join forces with the hill chiefs and to attack Anandpur. The combined forces laid siege to the city. After a long battle, the Mughal army offered safe passage to the Guru and his family. Guru Gobind, along with his family and men, left the city on 5-6 December 1705. The Guru instructed Gurbaksh, one of his Sikhs, to take care of the gurdwaras.

The Takhat Keshgarh Sahib is a beautiful marble edifice that was constructed between 1936-44 under the supervision of Sant Hari Singh Kaharpuri. It is built atop a hill and its sanctum sanctorum has the weapons of the Guru on display. These include the *khanda* used by Guru Gobind Singh to prepare the *amrit*, the *katar* and the *barchha* (spear) that belonged to the Guru. There is also the *barchha* of Bhai Bachittar Singh who drove away the drunken elephant of the enemy army. *Saif* believed to be of Caliph Ali (son-in-law of Prophet Mohammad) is also exhibited for the Darshan of the *sangat*. The *Saif* is said to have been presented to Guru Gobind Singh in the Fort of Agra by Emperor Bahadur Shah.

Guru Gobind Singh spent a quarter century at Anandpur Sahib. To protect the city from the attacks of hill chiefs and the Mughals, the Guru constructed five defensive forts around the town: Keshgarh at the centre, and others being Anandgarh (fort of bliss), Lohgarh (fort of steel), Holgarh (fort of colour), and Fatehgarh (fort of victory).

Gurdwara Qila Anandgarh Sahib is one of the five forts built by the Guru to defend Anandpur city. It is situated about 800 metres south-east of the Takhat Keshgarh Sahib; it had acted as the command centre for the Sikhs when attacked by the hill chiefs and the Mughals. The *baoli* at the gurdwara, which was completed in 1970, has 135 marbled steps. The water level of the old *baoli* is approached through a covered passage.

Gurdwara Qila Fatehgarh Sahib is situated on the northern outskirts of Anandpur, in the territory of Sahota village. While this fort was being constructed, Sahibzada Fateh Singh was born, hence it was named Qila Fatehgarh Sahib. 'Fatehgarh' means 'the fort of victory'.

Gurdwara Qila Lohgarh Sahib, situated one-and-a-half kilometres southwest of Takhat Sri Keshgarh Sahib, marks the site that was strategically built by the Guru to defend the city close to the river. It was the second strongest fort, and like Anandgarh, it acted as a deterrent to enemy attacks. In one of the battles, Bhai Bachchittar Singh used a *barchha* to engage with a drunken elephant that was sent by the hill chiefs to break the main gate of the fort. This is one of the weapons displayed at Takhat Sri Keshgarh Sahib. Also, it was here that the weapons were manufactured for the Sikh soldiers.

Gurdwara Holgarh Sahib is situated one-and-a-half kilometres northwest of the town, across the Charan Ganga rivulet. Guru Gobind, in the spring of 1701, began the tradition of celebrating 'Hola' on the day after Holi, the popular Hindu festival of colours. The Guru encouraged the Sikhs to use the day to demonstrate their warrior skills. To this day, thousands of Sikhs come together and participate in the celebrations. The occasion is concluded with a display of strength by the Nihangs and various other Sikh groups who come from all over the world to Holgarh Sahib. The main activities during the week-long celebrations are sword fighting, coil throwing, tent pegging, and horse riding.

Qila Taragarh is situated five kilometres away on the outskirts of Sri Anandpur Sahib. As it is located at the highest point overlooking the valley, it provided the Sikh soldiers a clear view of the approaching enemy from the Kahlur fort. Further ahead is the *baoli*, from where Bhai Kanhaya used to take water to serve those injured in the battle, including the injured of the enemy.

Since Guru Tegh Bahadur and Guru Gobind Singh spent significant amounts of time near Takhat Keshgarh Sahib; there are several gurdwaras that mark the various historic events related to the Gurus. **Gurdwara Bhora Sahib** marks the place where the ninth Guru resided as well as meditated. **Gurdwara Thara Sahib** is the place where the Guru heard the Kashmiri Brahmins and decided to go to Delhi. **Gurdwara Damdama Sahib** is also known as Takhat Sahib, as Guru Tegh Bahadur performed all the functions of the Akal Takhat from within its premises. It also acted like the court of the Guru, where he would receive important guests. Here, Guru Gobind Singh was installed as the Tenth Guru on 29 March 1676. In March 1698, the Guru summoned all the corrupt *masands* at Anandpur Sahib, where they were tried and punished.

Gurdwara Sis Ganj Sahib marks the site where the head of the ninth Master – Guru Tegh Bahadur – was cremated in November 1675. A platform within a small room was constructed where cremation was performed by Guru Gobind Singh himself. At the time of the evacuation of Anandpur in December 1705, Guru Gobind Singh especially entrusted it to the care of Gurbakhsh Udasi.

Gurdwara Mata Jito Ji is situated two kilometres northwest of Anandpur, marking the spot where Mata Jito was cremated in 1700.

The gurdwara associated with the young sahibzadas, four sons of the Gurus, is **Gurdwara Manji Sahib** which is also famous as Damalgarh. It is the place where the young sahibzadas grew up and received their training in martial arts. The place marks an incident when Sikhs commemorating battle between Ajmer Chand, the ruler of Bilaspur and the Sikhs. During the battle the flagbearer of the Sikhs, Bhai Maan Singh, Nischanchi got injured and Khalsa flag got broken. When the Guru was reported about the incident, he tore a piece of cloth from his Keski and set it in his turban declaring that from this time ahead Khalsa flag will never fall or get lowered. Sahibzada Fateh Singh also tore apart a piece of cloth on his turban.

A little drive away from the *takhat* is **Guru-Ka-Lahore.** Two trickling springs, claimed to be dug out from the stony mountain-side by Guru Gobind, exist here to this date.

Takhat Keshgarh Sahib was at the centre-stage when the Sikhs celebrated three centuries of the birth of the Khalsa in the year 1999. Millions of Sikhs as well as non-Sikhs gathered at this place to participate in the celebrations. This moment was fully utilized by the Takhat authorities in raising awareness among the people about the environment, and the authorities distributed plant saplings as prasad to millions. Also, a world-renowned architect, Moshe Safdei, was called upon to design the Khalsa Heritage Memorial Complex on a 100-acre site.

An aerial view of Takhat Keshgarh Sahib in Anandpur, Punjab. Home to many historical relics of
Guru Gobind Singh, Keshgarh Sahib is also the place where Khalsa Panth was born.

142

The historic Khanda *associated with the first Amrit ceremony undertaken by Guru Gobind Singh, 1699* AD *at Keshgarh Sahib, Anandpur.*
FACING PAGE: *Gurdwara Bhangani Sahib located near Paonta Sahib, where Guru Gobind Singh fought and won his first battle against the hill chiefs. Surrounding the gurdwara are now lush green fields.*

A historic baoli of Anandgarh Fort.

Gurdwara built in the memory of Bhai Jaita, who was later named as Bhai Jeewan Singh.

146

LEFT AND FACING PAGE: *Annual Hola Mohalla celebrations at Anandpur Sahib. Hola is a one-day Sikh festival that most often falls in March and takes place on the second day of the lunar month of Chett, a day after the Hindu spring festival of Holi. Hola Mohalla is a big festive event for Sikhs around the world.*

TAKHAT HAZUR SAHIB

In south-central India, on the banks of the River Godawari, is the Takhat Sri Hazur Sahib Abchal Nagar Sahib, 'the exalted presence'. The Mughal Emperor Bahadur Shah, while on his march to South India, was accompanied by Guru Gobind Singh. Both of them stayed at Nanded for a while and then the emperor proceeded towards Golconda, but the Guru continued to stay there. The Guru took many important decisions here regarding the community's future. He was injured when the Pathans, sent by the Wazir of Sirhind, attacked. Before his wounds could heal completely, the Guru got involved in archery, which proved fatal. He bestowed the Guruship on the Guru Granth Sahib on 6 October 1708. The Guru passed away the very next day, leaving behind his memories where now stand several gurdwaras.

In the Takhat Hazur Sahib Complex is situated the **Gurdwara Takhat Hazur Sahib,** which marks the place where Guru Gobind Singh breathed his last. This gurdwara was constructed on the orders of Maharaja Ranjit Singh. The main building is Angitha Sahib, where Guru Gobind Singh was cremated. The place has on display many relics that are associated with the Guru such as the *chakra* (quoit), the broad sword, the steel bow, the steel arrow, the *gurz* (heavy club with a large spherical knob), the small gilded *kirpan*, and five gilded swords. Every evening, thousands of Sikhs visit the sanctum sanctorum to catch a glimpse of these relics.

There are gurdwaras that mark the site of the Sikhs – men and women – who were loyal to the cause of the Guru. **Bunga Mai Bhago Ji** marks the site of Mai Bhago's residence. It is situated within the Gurdwara Takhat Sri Hazur Sahib complex.

The other site of significance of **Angitha Bhai Daya Singh** and **Dharam Singh** is associated with the two Panj Piaras. They took the Zafarnameh to Emperor Aurangzeb.

Gurdwara Hira Ghat Sahib is the spot where Guru Gobind Singh first set up camp on his arrival at Nanded, on the left bank of the River Godavari. As the tradition goes, one day Emperor Bahadur Shah, who came to call on him presented him with a diamond. The Guru threw it into the river. The emperor felt offended and thought that being a faqir, the Guru did not realize the value of the stone. The Guru invited the emperor to look into the water, who was astounded to witness numerous diamonds lying at the bottom of the river.

Gurdwara Mata Sahib marks the place where tents were pitched for Mata Sahib Devan, the Guru's wife, who had accompanied him during his journey to the south. Another gurdwara, **Shikar Ghat Sahib,** is situated on top of a hill where the Guru used to go for hunting excursions.

Gurdwara Nagina Ghat Sahib is on the left bank of the Godavari, and the incident connected with this shrine bears close similarity to that of Gurdwara Hira Ghat. Here, the Guru flung into the river a jewel presented by a Banjara Sikh. As the Guru asked him to look into the water, the merchant saw, to his amazement, many glittering jewels at the bottom of the river.

Gurdwara Baba Banda Bahadur Ghat Sahib marks the spot where Madho Das Bairagi used to live and meditate. He was renamed Banda Singh after he received the Khalsa rites by the Guru himself. There is an interesting incident by which the Guru was revealed to Banda Singh Bahadur. The Guru reached Madho Das's place on 3 September 1708, upon finding no one at home, the Guru sat on his cot. Madho Das was furious, but soon realized that it was the Guru who sat before him. He fell at the Guru's feet and submitted himself.

Gurdwara Mal Tekri Sahib is to the northeast of *takhat*, which derives its name from an old mound previously known as Chakri Mal, or Mal Tilla. It was here that the Guru unearthed a treasure. It is believed that the

ABOVE: Takhat Sri Hazur Sahib.
PRECEDING PAGES 148-149: Sikh Panj Piaras carrying Nishan Sahibs, leading a procession at Anandpur Sahib.

Guru came to know about the treasure through a fakir named Lakkar Shah.

Gurdwara Sangat Sahib marks that place where the treasure unearthed at Mal Tekri was brought and distributed by the Guru, not by counting the number of coins but by the amount that can be held in a shield. The shield that was used by the Guru is preserved here.

152

ABOVE: *Aarti being performed at the Takhat Hazur Sahib in Nanded, Maharashtra.* LEFT AND FACING PAGE: *Weapons of Guru Gobind Singh, the tenth Guru, being shown to the* sangat, *or congregation, at the Takhat Hazur Sahib in Nanded.*

FACING PAGE AND ABOVE: Kalagi *and* Panch Kala Shastra *of Guru Gobind Singh in the sanctum sanctorum of Takhat Sri Hazur Sahib, Nanded.*

157

Amrit sanchar ceremony at Takhat Sri Hazur Sahib, Nanded. Sikhs who have been through the Amrit Ceremony of initiation, or Amrit Sanchar, become baptized Sikhs, take new names, and wear the five Ks, the five things that Guru Gobind Singh commanded Khalsa Sikhs to wear (Kesh, Kangha, Kada, Kachera and Kirpan). The Amrit Ceremony is the initiation rite introduced by Guru Gobind Singh, when he founded the Khalsa in 1699.

158

ABOVE: Mai Bhagon's gun at Gurdwara Mal Tekri, Nanded.
BELOW LEFT: Dhal, *shield of Guru Gobind Singh at Gurdwara Mal Tekri, Nanded.*
RIGHT: Rare breed of Neela Ghodas believed to be from the lineage of the horses belonging to the tenth Guru Gobind Singh at Takhat Sri Hazur Sahib, Nanded.

ABOVE: Following an age old tradition, a sevadar carries a 'gaggar', a copper vessel filled with water from River Godavari to perform the cleaning of the sanctum sanctorum at Takhat Sri Hazur Sahib, Nanded.
BELOW: Ardaas, or prayer being performed at Takhat Sri Hazur Sahib, Nanded.

TAKHAT DAMDAMA SAHIB

Takhat Damdama Sahib is located in the village of Talwandi Sabo in the Bhatinda district of Punjab. Guru Gobind Singh stayed here for nine months in 1706, and took rest after engaging in prolonged battles against the Mughals and the hill chiefs. Earlier, Guru Tegh Bahadur had also stayed here. Before Guru Gobind's arrival at Talwandi, two of the Guru's sons were bricked alive at Sirhind and two laid down their lives at Chamkaur Sahib. The grief-stricken Guru chose this place to make it a centre of Sikh learning, and the Sikhs began flocking here from far and near.

It was at Damdama Sahib that Bhai Dalla was tested for his bravery. Chaudhary Dalla once boasted about his Jutt soldiers and subsequently Guru Gobind Singh asked him to provide a couple of his men as targets so that he could test the range and striking power of a weapon. The strange demand stunned Dalla and his men out of their wits, and none of them came forward. The Guru then called out two Rangreta Sikhs, who were at that moment busy tying their turbans. They came running, turbans in hand, each trying to outrun the other in order to be the first to face the bullet. Dalla, astonished at the Sikh spirit of sacrifice, was humbled.

Sacred relics including two swords, one muzzle-loading gun, a seal, and an old copy of the Guru Granth Sahib are preserved here in a domed cubicle behind the sanctum. Another relic, a mirror, said to have been presented to Guru Gobind Singh by the *sangat* of Delhi, is displayed in the hall. Of the two swords displayed here, one is believed to have belonged to Guru Gobind Singh and the other, heavy and double-edged, to Baba Deep Singh. The muzzle-loader is believed to be the one that Guru Gobind Singh received as a present. From here, the Guru moved further south to meet Emperor Bahadur Shah, whom he had helped to attain the throne of the Mughal Empire after the death of Aurangzeb.

Damdama Sahib was officially recognized as the fifth *takhat* on 18 November 1966.

The area around Damdama Sahib, as well as the complex itself, is marked with places associated with the Guru. **Gurdwara Manji Sahib Patshahi Nauvin** is dedicated to Guru Tegh Bahadur – it was from this spot that he used to supervise the digging of the tank, Gurusar. Guru Gobind Singh is believed to have had the tank de-silted and deepened.

Adjoining the Durbar Sahib is **Gurdwara Nivas Asthan Damdama Sahib Patshahi Nauvin,** a multi-storeyed octagonal tower, which marks the residence of Guru Gobind Singh. **Gurdwara Mata Sundri Ji** and **Gurdwara Mata Sahib Devan Ji**, mark the places where the holy ladies lived during their stay at Talwandi Sabo in 1706. Not far from here is **Gurdwara Likhansar**. According to Bhai Kuir Singh, there used to be a pool of water into which the Guru would throw reed-pens. Once, Bhai Dalla asked him why he did so? To quote the Sakhi Pothi, the Guru said: 'Thousands of Sikhs will hereafter study the holy texts in this place and then these pens will come into use. This is our Kashi (seat of learning); those who study here will cast off their ignorance and rise to be authors, poets, and commentators.'

Half a kilometre away is situated **Gurdwara Nanaksar,** where existed a natural pond. A little further is **Gurdwara Jandsar** that marks the place referred to as Jandiana in old chronicles; this is where the Guru distributed largesse to his Singhs.

Gurdwara Tibbi Sahib is close to a *sarovar* known as Mahalsar. This is where the Guru's Sikhs got training in mock battles. The site continues to be the venue for the traditional festivities during Hola Mohalla and Baisakhi.

Burj Baba Deep Singh is a 20-metre-high domed tower adjoining the north-east corner of the Takhat Sahib, It was constructed by Baba Deep Singh Shahid of the

A sevadar *at Takhat Damdama Sahib.*

Shahid *misl*. The well, which still supplies drinking water to the complex, was dug by Baba Deep Singh himself.

Gurdwara Samadh Bhai Dalla Singh marks the site where Chaudhary Dalla or Dall Singh – as he was known after receiving the vows of the Khalsa at the hands of Guru Gobind Singh – was cremated.

Gurdwara Thara Sahib Bhai Bir Singh and **Dhir Singh** marks the place where two Rangreta Sikhs offered themselves as targets for the Guru to test a muzzle-loading gun presented to him by a fellow Sikh.

Gurdwara Bunga Mastuana Sahib is not a historical shrine as such, but is a prestigious institution for training young scholars in the theory and practice of the Sikh faith.

The five *takhats* act like guardians for the Sikhs, keeping watchful eyes over the people and their doctrines. In today's tech-savvy world, more and more Sikhs living on different continents remain connected, thanks to the *takhats*. And due to this advancement in lifestyle, the role and meaning of the *takhats* will become even more valuable for the coming generations of Sikhs.

ABOVE: The muzzle-loader that Guru Gobind Singh received as a present.
FACING PAGE: Mirror from the sangat *of Delhi presented to Guru Gobind Singh ji.*
It is believed that praying while looking into it can cure face deformities.

CHAPTER IV

SEATS OF POWER
Forts and Fortresses

GURU HARGOBIND CHANGED THE FACE OF THE COMMUNITY BY INCORPORATING AND LEGITIMIZING THE IDEA OF TEMPORAL POWER IN THE SIKH IDEOLOGY. ANOTHER SIGNIFICANT CHANGE HE BROUGHT ABOUT WAS THE CREATION OF THE FIRST SIKH ARMY OF MOUNTED SOLDIERS WITH MATCHLOCK GUNS. THE SIKH ARMY FOUGHT WITH THE MUGHAL PROVINCIAL ARMY AND EMERGED VICTORIOUS. THE HOUSE OF THE GURUS, UNTIL GURU GOBIND SINGH, DID NOT ENVISAGE BUILDING FORTS TO DEFEND THE COMMUNITY AT ANANDPUR.

THE FORTRESSES AND FORTALICES BUILT BY GURU GOBIND SINGH NOT ONLY HOUSED AND PROTECTED SOLDIERS, EQUIPMENT AND SUPPLIES, BUT ALSO LAID THE FOUNDATION OF THE SIKH COMMUNITY'S FUTURE AS RULERS OF THE LAND. THE EARLIER GURUS HAD DESIGNED AND BUILT TOWNS WHERE THE SIKH ETHOS WAS INTRODUCED AS WELL AS GROOMED. THE FORTS FURTHER DEFINED THE MESSAGE OF THE GURUS AMONGST THE COMMUNITY. THE PRESENCE OF THE FORTS WAS NOT NEW TO THE LANDSCAPE OF PUNJAB, BUT FOR THE FIRST TIME, IT WAS A RELIGIOUS LEADER WHO ENVISAGED THE IDEA. THEY SAFEGUARDED THE PRACTITIONERS OF THE SIKH IDEOLOGY FROM ATTACKS AND ALSO ASSISTED IN THE CRYSTALLIZATION OF THE THOUGHT PROCESSES OF THE KHALSA FAITH. AS THE SIKHS GREW IN STRENGTH, NUMBER AND POWER, THEY TOOK OVER MANY EXISTING, FAMOUS AND HISTORIC FORTS AND MADE THEM THEIR OWN.

THE FIELD FORTIFICATION PLANNED BY THE GURU WAS CRUCIAL TO DOMINATE DEFENSIVE ACTION BECAUSE IT FORMED A LESS OBVIOUS TARGET FOR THE ENEMY. THE DEFENCE LINE COULD BE RE-ESTABLISHED RELATIVELY QUICKLY IN CASE THE ENEMY PENETRATED THE FRONT LINE. ALSO, IN CASE THE SIKHS WERE FORCED TO PULL BACK OR WERE OVERRUN, THE SECOND LINE BEHIND THEM COULD TAKE OVER THE DEFENCE FAIRLY QUICK. THE GURU POSITIONED HIS ARMY KEEPING IN MIND HOW RAPIDLY AN ENEMY FORCE COULD PROGRESS IN THE TERRAIN. THE SIKH FORTS WERE NOT USED AS PLATFORMS FOR TERRITORIAL EXPANSION OR POLITICAL DOMINATION.

FACING PAGE: A painting of Maharaja Karam Singh in Qila Mubarak, Patiala.

It was not until the eighteenth century that the Sikhs had become the rulers of the land and felt the need to have forts to expand their political domination over Punjab. The oldest among these forts that the Sikhs took control of was that of Bhatinda. The fort, made of small bricks, dates to the second century of the Christian era, when Dab, a Hindu king, got it constructed along with the Kushana king Kanishka. The fort is famous since the first woman ruler of India – Razia Sultan – was incarcerated here. During the decline of the Mughals in the eighteenth century, the fort came under the control of Ala Singh of Patiala. It was renamed Gobindgarh Fort by Maharaja Karam Singh of Patiala to commemorate the visit of Guru Gobind Singh.

Baba Ala Singh established the kingdom of Patiala amidst the decline of the Mughal Empire, from a petty zamindari of thirty villages, especially during the times of Banda Singh Bahadur. He was the grandson of Chaudhary Phul, whose son – Ram Singh – was baptized by Guru Gobind Singh. In 1763, Baba Ala Singh decided to build the fort in Patiala, now famous as Qila Androon in the Qila Mubarak complex. It was the principal residence of the royal family of Patiala. It has an imposing gate and distinct buildings: Topkhana, Qila Mubarak, Sheesh Mahal, Toshakhana, and the Prison. Between the Qila Androon and the outer walls is situated the secretariat and the Durbar Hall that was constructed by Maharaja Karam Singh. The Durbar Hall houses a rare collection of Belgium-cut-glass chandeliers. There are also rare arms and armaments displayed here. The rooms in the Qila are beautifully painted with frescoes and are intricately decorated with mirror work in Kangra style on the walls.

MAHARAJA NARENDRA SINGH

The Moti Bagh palace, constructed in 1847 by Maharaja Narendra Singh, was designed on the pattern of Shalimar gardens of Lahore with Sheesh Mahal, terraces and a beautifully laid garden. The four-storeyed structure of the palace is a historical marvel as it houses rare attractions for all. A very learned Maharaja Narendra Singh successfully made Patiala a centre of art. He patronized many artists, litterateurs, and musicians. The epitome of his endeavours is depicted in renditions by artists in Sheesh Mahal, where the poetry of Keshav, Surdas and Bihari are beautifying the inner walls and ceilings. The themes embody Raga Ragini, Nayak-Nayika and Baramasa in the Rajasthani style. The most intricate is the finely laid mirror work and floral work. The museum houses a rich collection of miniature paintings of the nineteenth century depicting *Geet Gobinda* and Jaya Deva's poetry. The palace houses the world's largest collection of medals awarded to Maharaja Bhupinder Singh. Some of the rarest are the Order of the Garter (England) of 1348 A.D., the Order of the Golden Fleece (Austria) founded in 1430 A.D., the Order of St. Andrews (Russia) founded in 1688 by Peter the Great; the Order of the Rising Sun (Japan); the Order of the Double Dragon (China), and the Order of the White Elephant (Thailand). There are medals that were instituted by the Maharaja himself. There are various kinds of exclusive furniture items from Burma and Kashmir, and rare manuscripts such as *Janamsakhis Gulistan* and *Bostan* by Sheikh Saadi of Shiraz, which were acquired by the Mughal Emperor Shah Jahan. There is also a collection of rare coins from which one could understand numismatic history. The most magnificent aspect of the edifice is a huge tank that has a suspension rope bridge similar to those in Rishikesh.

The fort of Bahadurgarh is another stately and imposing edifice that was built at the instance of Maharaja Karam Singh to mark the visit of Guru Tegh Bahadur. The Guru came to the place at the invitation of Saif Khan, a relative of Aurangzeb, the Mughal emperor. The fort has a gurdwara inside the building and one across the road. Two circular ramparts surround the fort. There is a moat that is 25 feet deep and 58 feet wide and 29 feet high. The fort structure needs attention, as many of its frescoes are damaged; moreover it has a huge potential to attract tourists if conserved to its pristine glorious past.

MAHARAJA RANJIT SINGH

Ranjit Singh (1780-1839), the Maharaja of Punjab, ruled over a region extending from the Khyber Pass in the west to the River Sutlej in the east, from the Kashmir in the north to Sindh in the south. He engaged with Shah Zaman, the king of Kabul and grandson of Ahmad Shah Durrani, and challenged him openly in Lahore. On the departure of the Afghan from the canvas of Lahore, he moved into the city of Lahore and took charge of the Lahore Fort in 1799. The taking over of the city of Lahore and the fort was significant for the history of the Sikhs. It was the biggest fort of the region and had the legacy of Mughal domination for many years. It had been the provincial capital of Punjab and its architecture reached its epitome during the times of Akbar, Jahangir, Shah Jahan, and Aurangzeb. All of them added new buildings to the fort. As a city, Lahore has deep-rooted connections with Sikh history. Guru Nanak visited the city, Guru Ramdas was born there, Guru Arjan was tortured and martyred there, and Guru Hargobind visited the city several times. There were many campaigns sent from Lahore to curb the Sikhs. Many Sikhs were captured and killed in Nakhas khana. There are many historic shrines such as – Gurdwara Patshahi Pehli, Gurdwara Janam Asthan Guru Ramdas, Dharamshala Guru Ramdas, Gurdwara Dehra Sahib, Shahid Ganj Mani Singh ji, Samadh of Maharaja Ranjit Singh – which together are the Sikh historical moments in Lahore.

Once Maharaja Ranjit Singh took over the Lahore Fort, he began giving shape to one of the most successful empires in the world. The fort once again became the centre of grandeur. Ordaining the world's most precious Koh-i-Noor diamond, Ranjit Singh would dress in white robes and surround himself with nobility, from all religious faiths and nationalities. Golden pillars covered the three parts of the Durbar Hall; rich shawl carpets, embroidered in gold and silver, covered the floors. All those who visited the fort were treated with dignity and respect. The splendour of the Lahore durbar was best expressed during diplomatic and ceremonial occasions. All the daily business was carried on inside the Lahore Fort at Mussamman Burj. A public court, Diwan-e-Aam was held until noon. Maharaja Ranjit Singh presided over the meetings with princes, nobles, kardars, and heard reports from his messengers scattered across the subcontinent. The fort was also witness to the festivities of Baisakhi, Dussehra, Basant, Holi, and Diwali.

Maharaja Ranjit Singh understood the value of forts, hence within no time began spreading his control over the major forts of the Punjab. One such fort was that of Multan. The city and the fort were at the centre of the province under Mughal rule, and then was taken over by the Afghans under the leadership of Ahmad Shah Durrani in 1752. With the expansion of the Sikh *misls*, the fort came under the control of the Bhangi *misl* for a while before it was taken over by the Afghans. Ranjit Singh made many expeditions to the city before he could take control of the fort. He eventually got his heart's desire, but not before a gruesome, bloody battle with the Afghans in 1818. The fort was witness to Diwan Mul Raj's revolt against the British in 1848-49. The fort, situated on a hill in the city, was severely damaged during the attacks by the British. It is believed that the walls were very high, flanked by thirty towers, and enclosed numerous houses and even a mosque. The circumference of the fort was two kilometres, with two towers at each of the four gates, and a moat that was 25 feet deep and 40 feet wide. At a considerable elevation stands a citadel and there is also an ancient Hindu temple.

The control of the fort of Jamrud at Khyber Pass, on the western border in the Northwest Frontier Province of

Pakistan, was crucial to keep Lahore safe against attacks from the western borders. The fort was built at the insistence of Maharaja Ranjit Singh with the objective to stop the attacks from Afghanistan. In 1837, Hari Singh Nalwa lost his life defending this fort. Due to this strategically located fort, Punjab could focus on progress and development.

In 1807, due to the international pressure on Great Britain, incurred by the conclusion of the Treaty of Tilsit between Napolean Bonaparte and the Czar of Russia, there was a threat of a Franco-Russian invasion of India. The British wisely decided to make Ranjit Singh an ally and agreed to have River Sutlej as the border. It became vital for the Maharaja to have a fort built on the western bank of the river. The British had constructed the Ludhiana fort on the eastern bank of the river. It was both a diplomatic and military necessity. Maharaja Ranjit Singh, on the other hand, reconstructed the Phillaur Fort after renovating an existing Mughal caravan *serai*, to serve as the last outpost of his empire in the East and the first entry point for all visitors and representatives of the British. The fort had a distinctly European character, thanks to the French generals at the service of Ranjit Singh, who gave the latter advice about the construction. An extensive moat was dug as a last-ditch defence stratergy, and the outer walls were inwardly inclined to facilitate the deflection of cannon balls. Governor Mohkam Chand's strong forces were stationed at Phillaur from 1808 to 1812. The fort never faced any battle situation but served as an important centre of Ranjit Singh's military aptitude.

GOBINDGARH

Within a decade of his rule, Maharaja Ranjit Singh's state had become a rich kingdom. He modified a fortress built by a Bhangi Sandhu Jat into a fort known as Gobindgarh. The fort was converted into an artillery depot and also housed a treasury, which was home to the world famous Koh-i-Noor diamond. The fort is based on a square pattern, comprising red bricks layered with lime, with a parametre of 1500 square metre with two strong gates, four large bastions and a well-defined rampart. The regal main entrance is called Nalwa Gate, after the great Sikh General Hari Singh Nalwa and the other gate is known as Keelar Gate. There were 25 cannons on the ramparts and a treasury towards the centre of the fort. Fakir Imamuddin was appointed the first Qiladar of the fort, and Misr Beli Ram was given charge of the treasury. Special provisions were made to store large amounts of grains and rations for the 12,000-strong Maharaja's army. For a good number of years, the fort was under the rule of the British army, and then after 1947, under the rule of the Indian army. During partition, many refugees were also given shelter here. The fort was visited by the Viceroy of India, George Eden, the Earl of Auckland, along with his sister Emily Eden, the English novelist and poet. This visit is well documented in her memoirs titled *Up the Country*. During their visit she wrote that 'whosoever gets hold of Gobindgarh at his death will also get hold of his kingdom'. She mentions two golden chairs that were placed on the roof of the *deorhi*, one for the Maharaja and the other for the Viceroy. She also left memorable sketches of the Maharaja and his nobles. The fort was used by the Maharaja not only as his residence but also to receive state guests, as well as to attend to important administrative matters of the empire. It would not be any exaggeration to say that this fort held centre-stage in Punjab politics for many years.

KAPURTHALA

While driving from Delhi to the Golden Temple in Amritsar – one is wonderstruck by the spectacular architecture of Kapurthala. Designed by the French Architect M. Marcel, the edifices emulate the same energy as the captivating palaces of Versailles and Fontainebleau – the epitome of French architecture.

Jassa Singh Ahluwalia was the founder of the kingdom of Kapurthala. Born in the village of Ahlu, near Lahore, his family was blessed by Guru Hargobind. After the death of his father, Sardar Badar Singh Sandhu in 1723 AD, his mother gave him under the care of Mata Sundari, the widow of Guru Gobind Singh. He grew up learning Sikh scriptures from Bhai Mani Singh. About warfare and administration, he received his lessons from Nawab Kapur Singh. In 1748 AD, during the Sarbat Khalsa, Nawab Kapur Singh, appointed Jassa Singh as his successor, and awarded him the title of Sultan e Qaum, 'king of the community'. It was a crucial moment for Punjab as it was beginning to witness brutal attacks by the ferocious Ahmad Shah. He attacked nine times and defeated the Marathas in the third Battle of Panipat. He had realized that the Sikh power would have to be curbed, and he mobilized his forces to take action against the community in 1762. Abdali's forces snuck up on and massacred a Sikh caravan comprising old men, women and children. It is believed that over 20,000 Sikhs lost their lives on 5 February 1762. This incident is known as Wada Ghullughara, or 'the great holocaust'. The massacre did not demoralize the Sikhs, and within no time, under the capable leadership of Jassa Singh Ahluwalia, they began establishing their hegemony over the Mughal's important stronghold of Sirhind. By the month of November, the Sikhs had gained Amritsar. The Afghan ruler was in no mood to let the Sikhs dig their roots deep, and sent a peace emissary proposing a treaty, and when that was declined by the Sikhs, Ahmed Shah sent his forces. A battle between the two camps was fought in October 1762, and resulted in the Sikhs having to retreat into lakhi jungles.

The Sikh *misls* realized that they would have to put forward a cohesive front against the enemy power, and hence they decided to consider Jassa Singh Ahluwalia as the leader of their joint army. He, along with the Dal Khalsa, led the Sikhs to many victorious campaigns. He

settled in Kapurthala and died in Amritsar in 1783 AD. He was issueless, and hence was succeeded by Bhag Singh, whose son Fateh Singh Ahluwalia became a close ally of Ranjit Singh.

Fateh Singh Ahluwalia was a wise ruler, who played his cards well. He entered into a treaty with the British East India Company in 1806. He was a considered a brother by Ranjit Singh, but in 1826, he decided to step back quietly, keeping his focus on the development and growth of his city. His successor, S. Nihal Singh, sustained the process of growth. In 1852, Nihal Singh died and his son Raja Randhir Singh took charge. Randhir Singh actively participated in the 1857 Mutiny along with the British forces. Nihal Singh's son – Maharaja Kharak Singh – ruled the state from 1870 to 1877. The Maharaja's son, Tikka Jagatjit Singh (1872–1948), took over the throne at the tender age of five. He received the best of education, and was well-versed in French, English, Punjabi, Persian, and Urdu. He probably was one of the most widely travelled Indian kings of his time. He had been all over Europe, North, Central and South America, Egypt, China, Japan, Siam, Java and the Straits settlement. His wide experiences led him to introduce massive projects in the city that were to permanently mark Kapurthala on the world map. Because of his concerted efforts, the city became an example in regards to health and sanitation. He was passionate about the monumental scale, and the symmetry of French architecture, art, style especially of the period of Louis XIV. He appointed French architect M. Marcel for the project of building his palace on the lines of Elysee Palace, the current palace of the President of France. The original intent was to use red stones; however, due to the budget constraints the edifice was finished in pink plaster of Paris. The palace echoes many aspects of the Palace of Versailles as it reflects the Renaissance style of architecture. Many skilled artisans were engaged from India and Europe to do the interiors of the palace that took approximately eight years to complete; i.e. it finished in 1908. The great Durbar Hall witnessed the epitome of Kapurthala royalty's hospitality for esteemed guests from all over the world. The interest of Maharaja to construct buildings was not only limited to palaces. Some of the fine examples of his interest in the various architectural styles are that of Moorish Mosque, the gurdwara at Kapurthala, and the gurdwara at Sultanpur Lodhi. The Moorish Mosque is believed to be a replica of the grand mosque of Marakesh, Morocco, and was designed by the French architect, Monsieur M Manteaux. It was commissioned by Maharaja Jagatjit Singh and took 13 years to complete. The mosque's inner dome contains decorations by the artists of the Mayo School of Art, Lahore. The gurdwara of Kapurthala is a large imposing red stone building built in Indo-Sarcenic style. The Gurdwara Ber Sahib situated at Sultanpur Lodhi marks the historic site where Guru Nanak spent 14 years of his life and also attained enlightenment. The place has a *ber*, or jujube tree under which it is believed that the Guru uttered the *mool mantra*.

The royal houses of Nabha, Faridkot, Jind and Malerkotla were all blessed with the Guru's visits. The forts, palaces and royal gardens in these cities are unique and reflect distinct architecture.

It is important that the people associated with Punjab begin to realize the worth of its matchless heritage. The beautiful architecture marvels that it possesses are not only worthy of architectural studies but also need to be brought to the forefront of India's tourist map. The state is well situated geographically so as not to miss the golden opportunity to be on the world heritage sites map.

CONCLUSION

Sikh heritage places and objects continue to play a significant role in the lives of most Sikhs due to the natural, historic and traditional ideals linked to them and their surrounding landscapes. Irrespective of the brutal assaults of history faced by the Sikhs – such as the partition of Punjab – they have still maintained the merit of their inaccessible heritage.

The Sikh shrines that a large number of Sikhs left behind in the newly formed Pakistan in 1947, never left their thoughts. The shrines and the desire to visit and manage them as per the traditions set by the Gurus have been in every Sikh's daily prayers. The places and the objects of the Sikh community remain an influential denominator in the progression of the Sikhs world over. Nevertheless, the neglect of the preservation and conservation of the objects and places cannot be ignored.

The Sikh Diaspora that is spread over the world and thrives economically, always took the word of the Guru along. This work has tried to capture the relics that, having survived the wraths and glorification that history offers, are a prime witness to the establishment of the Sikh community. Most of the heritage objects associated with the Sikh Gurus that are covered in the book are in private collections or in gurdwaras, but as demonstrated, need professional help in order to be conserved.

The Harmandir Sahib is visited by people from all over the world. In the last decade, new gold plates have been put on the structure along with other conservation efforts. The procedure was distinct from the earlier occasion because at this time the *sangat* played the dominant role and contributed large quantities of gold unlike earlier when Maharaja Ranjit Singh contributed the entire amount. The Harmandir complex and the area surrounding it needs all that could possibly be done to conserve it. Similarly, the five *takhats* that bind the Sikhs into a moral order, with powers to decree *hukamnamas*, are places where the objects have the Gurus' touch. The edifices, the alleys and the objects lying in *takhats* such as Patna Sahib are still in condition that could be well preserved for generations to come. During our visits to the forts of Punjab, we realized that many of these may not even survive if corrective conservational action is not taken promptly.

Another facet, as the beautiful photographs have depicted, is that it is worth for the government and the civil society to pay attention to Punjab as a new tourist sector. The grandeur of the *Ajooba* is an example of modern architecture embracing the Sikh values and traditions, and similarly, the forts such as Qila Mubarak, or the cities such as Kapurthala, need to be on the top of the agenda of India's tourism. The experiencing of the objects and the edifices exposes one to the fact that the preservation and conservation of the same are not part of the active agenda of the Sikhs or state politics; hence the concern of loosing those looms large until something is done promptly.

There is no denying the fact that there has been an increase in the recognition of the cultural landscape of Punjab, but there is a further need of on-ground management of historical edifices and objects. Also, there is a necessity to have an integrated approach towards managing heritage projects by including more experts in Conservation Architecture – hopefully reducing the pattern of demolishing traditional old buildings and coming up with buildings that are totally covered by marble.

The work has also endeavoured to bring to light the buildings and collections in private hands by exposing broad classifications of collections in museums, libraries, monuments, and sites. The families have kept these for generations. Some of them are kept in the best possible ways but many require the community's assistance to be saved. The need is to have public and private partnership at all levels. The Sikh Heritage needs to be integrated with state processes across all areas of heritage, so that they become integrated in education, tourism, and community associations. The success of these processes will help attain economic and social benefits for the community and the state.

The Sikh Heritage traces the history of valour and devotion. This heritage needs to be valued and conserved, through communication and provision of services so that the objects and sites show Sikhs as strong allies. If preservation is done as indicated, then the valour and devotion of the Sikhs towards their faith will become a unique example of understanding the past experiences in an efficacious way for the world.

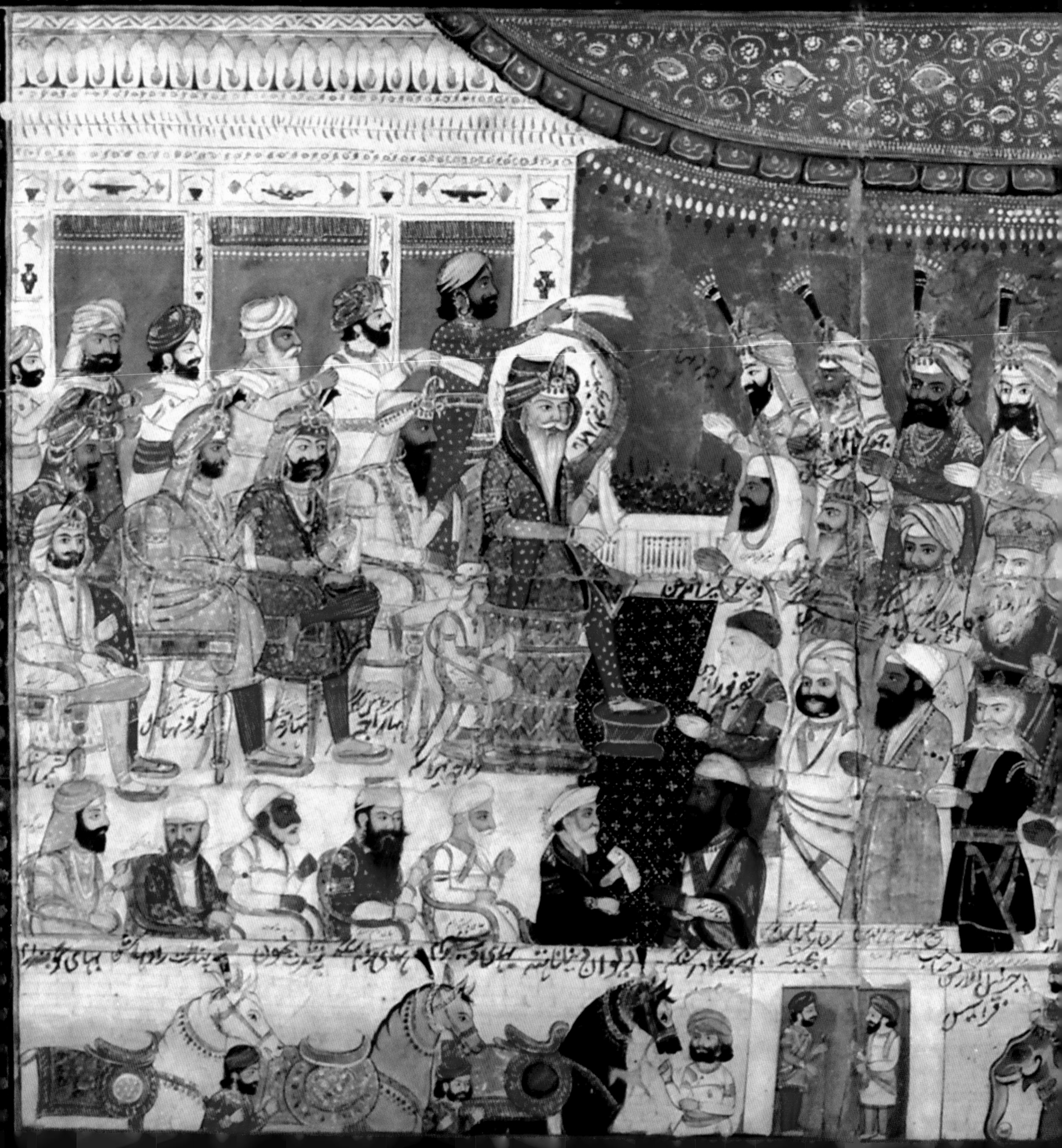

A miniature painting of the Durbar, Court of Maharaja Ranjit Singh in Lahore, with Maharaja Ranjit Singh sitting on his golden throne along with his durbaris, or courtiers. Each courtier's name is written along with their painting.

173

174

LEFT: *Portrait of Maharaja Dalip Singh, the youngest son of Maharaja Ranjit Singh.*
RIGHT: *Portrait of Maharani Jinda, mother of Maharaja Dalip Singh.*
FACING PAGE: *A portrait of Maharaja Ranjit Singh (courtesy Maharaja Ranjit Singh Museum).*

ABOVE AND FACING PAGE: A set of miniature and rare paintings of Raja Sher Singh, Hira Singh and Rani Jinda.

ABOVE AND FACING PAGE: Horse of Maharaja Ranjit Singh, Leili; chieftains and a set of 12 miniatures of the Maharaja and his nobles and generals, in oval format (courtesy Maharaja Ranjit Singh Museum).

180

LEFT, ABOVE & BELOW: *Paintings of Sikh nobility from Maharaja Ranjit Singh Museum, Amritsar.*
RIGHT: *Commander-in-chief of Sikh Khalsa Army, Hari Singh Nalwa taking Guard of Honour at Jamrood Fort, Attock.*

181

ABOVE: A decorated chair from the durbar of Maharaja Ranjit Singh (courtesy Maharaja Ranjit Singh Museum).
ABOVE RIGHT: A rare shield depicting a Sikh soldier's encounter with a lion (courtesy Faqir Khana Museum).
RIGHT: Sword with grey jade hilt with portrait of Maharaja Ranjit Singh
(courtesy Maharaja Ranjit Singh Museum).

ABOVE AND FACING PAGE: *Military Manual of Maharaja Ranjit Singh's army (courtesy Maharaja Ranjit Singh Museum).*

Maharaja Ranjit Singh's sowaree, *cast in silver from the last of the survivors of Maharaja Ranjit Singh's family, Princess Bamba Sutherland's Collection (courtesy Fort Museum, Lahore).*

186

Shalimar Bagh in Lahore, which was used for Maharaja Ranjit Singh's grandson Naunihal Singh's wedding reception.
RIGHT: *Zamazama Gun that was won by Maharaja Ranjit Singh from the Bhagi misls in 1802. He used the gun during the siege of Multan.*
FACING PAGE: *A panoramic view from the Gurdwara of Maharaja Ranjit Singh at Lahore Fort showing Badshahi Masjid, Gurdwara Dera Sahib, Samadh of Maharaja Ranjit Singh, and Naulakha Building.*

188

The Phillaur Fort is also known as the Maharaja Ranjit Singh Fort, after the man who ruled Punjab between the years 1799 and 1839. The fort, now turned into a police academy, is on the banks of River Sutlej, near the Grand Trunk Road

189

Fountain and gardens of the Villa Palace, Kapurthala.
FACING PAGE: *Front view of Jagatjit Palace Kapurthala. It was, once upon a time, the home of Maharaja Jagatjit Singh, the main architect of modern-day Kapurthala. The Maharaja's palace and gardens were modelled on Versailles. He hired a French architect M. Marcel, who was inspired by the palaces of Versailles and Fontainbleau. Its POP figures and painted ceilings represent the finest features of French art and architecture. It was built in the Renaissance style with the sunken park in the front (known as Baija) and has many other similarities to the Palace of Versailles. The construction of this palace took roughly eight years (1900–1908). The interior decoration of the palace, which is unique of its kind in India, was carried out by expert European and Indian workmen. The great Durbar Hall is one of the finest in India. The palace is full of imported art work from France, Italy, and Holland.*

The Central Hall of Jagatjit Palace, Kapurthala is now being used as the library of Sainik School. It is decorated with portraits, artwork, and chandeliers.
FACING PAGE: *Wooden floor beautifully decorated with flower patterns and the crest of the royal family of Kapurthala.*

LEFT: *The Panj Mandir of Kapurthala, which has undergone massive expansion work.* RIGHT: *A church in Kapurthala.*
FACING PAGE: *A spectacular example of the secular history of Kapurthala is the Moorish Mosque,*
a famous replica of the Grand Mosque of Marakesh, Morocco, which was built by a French architect, Monsieur
M. Manteaux. Its construction was commissioned by the last ruler of Kapurthala, Maharaja Jagatjit Singh,
and took 13 years, from 1917 to 1930, to complete.

Inside of the grand Kapurthala Palace. The historic building now houses the District Courts.

197

198

*Qila Mubarak, a majestic fort located in the city of Bhatinda since 1100-1200 AD. The fort was visited by
Guru Nanak Dev, Guru Tegh Bahadur and Guru Gobind Singh and has a gurdwara marking these visits.*

Grand Entrance of the Qila Mubarak, Bhatinda.

199

LEFT: *Moti Bagh Palace, now turned into the National Institute of Sports. The palace was built as one of the largest residences in the world and served as principal residence of the Patiala royal family.*
BELOW: *A European-style fountain, Moti Bagh Palace, Patiala.*

Richly decorated with mirror work on walls and ceiling, the Qila Androon inside Qila Mubarak.
FACING PAGE: An aerial view of the entrance of Qila Mubarak, around which the historic town of Patiala developed.
Qila Mubarak was built by Ala Singh, founder of the Patiala dynasty in 1763.
FOLLOWING PAGES (204–205): Mirrored walls in the Sheesh Mahal, Motibagh Palace, Patiala.

ABOVE: Historic gun displayed at Bahadurgarh Fort. The fort, on the outskirts of Patiala, was built in the seventeenth century by Nawab Saif Khan during the reign of Aurangzeb and was called Saifabad. It was renamed by Maharaja Karam Singh of Patiala in the nineteenth century after the ninth Sikh Guru, Guru Tegh Bahadur, stayed here.

LEFT: *A Mazar of Sufi saint Pir Abdullah in Phillaur fort is visited by large number of devotees everyday.*

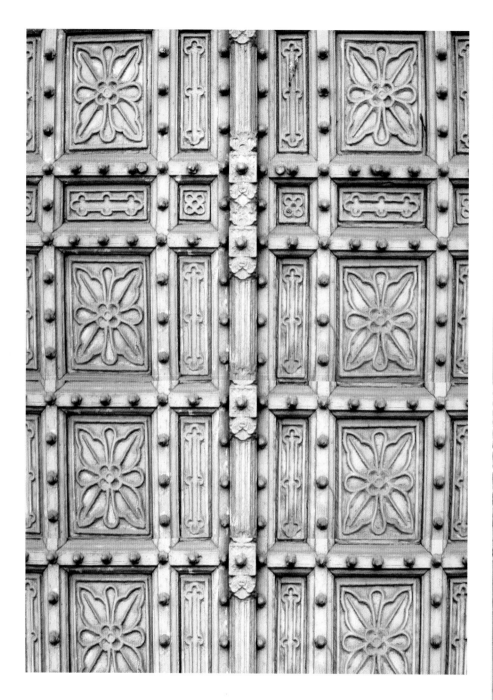

208

ABOVE: The workmanship on the wooden doors of the havelis is considered the finest example of the time.
RIGHT: Descendants of Sham Singh Attariwala, on of the illustrious generals of Maharaja Ranjit Singh's army. Behind can be seen the Samadhs of the Attari family near Amritsar.

INDEX OF IMPORTANT GURDWARAS

GURDWARA AJITGARH SAHIB is associated with Sahibzada Ajit Singh, who arrived here with 100-soldier strong cavalry. The place plays an important role in the Hola Mohalla celebrations, when various Sikh groups demonstrate their martial skills.

GURDWARA BANGLA SAHIB is associated with Guru Har Krishan. The gurdwara was built by the Sikh General, Sardar Bhagel Singh in 1783, who supervised the construction of nine Sikh shrines in Delhi in the same year, during the reign of Mughal Emperor, Shah Alam II.

GURDWARA BABA GURDITTA marks the place where Baba Gurditta ji, father of Guru Har Rai ji settled and spent time meditating.

GURDWARA BARI SANGAT, Kolkata was visited by Guru Nanak Dev and Guru Tegh Bahadur Sahib during their travels to the region. On his return journey from Dacca to Punjab, Guru Nanak is said to have stayed at this place and hence a gurdwara was built here. It is said that Guru Tegh Bahadur also stayed here during his journey to Bengal and Assam.

GURDWARA BHORA SAHIB marks the place where Guru Tegh Bahadur meditated for over 26 years. It was here that Makhan Shah found the Guru of the Sikhs.

GURDWARA BIBANGARH SAHIB in Fatehgarh is the place where the bodies of martyred Mata Gujri, Sahibzadas Zorawar Singh and Fateh Singh were kept.

GURDWARA BIBANGARH SAHIB marks the place in Kiratpur Sahib where Guru Gobind Singh came to take with respect the severed head of Guru Tegh Bahadur, brought by Bhai Jaita, to Anandpur Sahib.

GURDWARA CHARAN KANWAL marks the site of the garden where Guru Gobind Singh had a sip of water and a spell of brief sleep. It was here that his three devotees Bhai Mani Singh, Bhai Daya Singh, and Bhai Dharam Singh joined him.

GURDWARA CHEVIN PATSHAHI marks the place where Guru Hargobind gave his discourse on the relation between Bhakti and Shakti.

GURDWARA DAMDAMA SAHIB is associated with the 10th Sikh Guru, Guru Gobind Singh. It commemorates his meeting with Prince Muazzam, later known as Emperor Bahadur Shah, in 1707.

GURDWARA DURBAR SAHIB at Khadur Sahib marks the place associated with Guru Angad Dev, who breathed his last here. This place also marks the visits of Guru Hargobind, Guru Har Rai, and Guru Tegh Bahadur.

GURDWARA FATEHGARH SAHIB marks the place where the martyrdom of the younger sons of Guru Gobind Singh, Sahibzada Fateh Singh and Sahibzada Zorawar Singh, took place. It also marks the place that Banda Singh Bahadur conquered and razed the fort to ground.

GURDWARA GOBINDPURA in Ambala marks the place where the Guru had stopped to preach the message of God.

GURDWARA GURU ARJAN DEV SAHIB, Bilga marks the place where Guru Arjan Dev travelled from Goindwal Sahib and arrived here on 1 July 1589.

GURDWARA GURU KA LAHORE is located 12 kilometres north of Anandpur Sahib. It marks the place where the marriage of Guru Gobind took place after the Guru could not visit Lahore.

GURDWARA GURU KA MAHAL marks the place of the birth of Guru Tegh Bahadur in Amritsar.

GURDWARA GURU NANAKSAR SAHIB is located 10 km from Takhat Hazur Sahib. Guru Nanak Dev ji stopped here on his way to Bidar. He meditated for 9 days and 9 hours under the jujube tree.

GURDWARA KHADUR SAHIB is situated in Khadur Sahib in Tarn Taran district. It marks the place visited by eight Gurus. Guru Angad Dev ji lived here and was served by Guru Amar Das during his stay. Baba Budha ji also spent 12 years here.

GURDWARA MAL AKHARA marks the place where Guru Angad Dev ji gave religious discourses and developed the Gurmukhi script.

GURDWARA MATA GUJRI marks the place where the two younger sons of Guru Gobind Singh were detained in a high tower along with Mata Gujri at Fatehgarh Sahib, Sirhind.

GURDWARA GURUSAR PAKKA SAHIB PATSHAHI NAUVIN, Handiya marks the place where Guru Tegh Bahadur came in 1665 AD and rested near a pond. He blessed the pond, the water of which was used by the villagers to cure various ailments.

GURDWARA LAKHPAT SAHIB is located in the fort town of Lakhpat in Kutch, Gujarat. Several personal belongings of Guru Nanak's, like his wooden footwear can be seen here.

GURDWARA MAL TEKRI SAHIB is located 5 kms away from the city of Nanded. Guru Nanak visited this place in 1512 AD. Later, it was here that Guru Gobind Singh distributed the money among his army.

GURDWARA MATA SAHIB DEVAN is located close to Gurdwara Hira Ghat that Guru Gobind Singh visited.

GURDWARA HOLGARH SAHIB, Anandpur Sahib. It is here that Guru Gobind Singh introduced celebration of Hola Mohalla where the Sikhs demonstrated their skills in arms.

GURDWARA LOH GARH SAHIB, built in memory of the sixth guru, Guru Hargobind Sahib, is located where Lohgarh Fort built by the Guru once stood. The battle of Amritsar between Guru Hargobind and an imperial force, under Mukhlis Khan, was fought here in May 1629.

GURDWARA MANJI SAHIB marks the site where Diwan, congregation, was organized. It is here that a follower of Dhir Mal attempted the assassination of Guru Tegh Bahadur, but the Guru was saved.

GURDWARA MATA SUNDRI The Delhi Gurdwara Committee constructed this shrine on the site of the Haveli, where Mata Sundri, the first wife of Guru Gobind Singh stayed after the departure of the Guru to Deccan. It is believed that Mata Sundari nurtured and guided the Sikhs of Delhi for forty years after the Guru's death.

GURDWARA JYOTI SWAROOP is located a mile to the east of Gurdwara Fatehgarh Sahib and marks the spot where Mata Gujri, Sahibzadas Zorawar Singh and Fateh Singh, were cremated.

GURDWARA MAJNU-KA-TILLA is situated on the bank of River Jamuna in Delhi. The birth of Khalsa is celebrated here with much festivity. This gurdwara was constructed by Baghel Singh, a Sikh military leader.

GURDWARA MANJI SAHIB is located in Ambala where sixth and tenth Sikh Gurus stayed during their visit to Ambala.

GURDWARA MOTI BAGH is associated with Guru Gobind Singh, who camped at this site during his first visit to Delhi in 1707.

GURDWARA NAGINA GHAT is close to Takhat Hazur Sahib. When a merchant gave a precious stone to the Guru, he threw the stone in the river, completely shocking the merchant. The Guru asked him to pick the precious stone from the river, the merchant saw many stones in the river.

GURDWARA NANAK PIAO is a historical gurdwara located in north Delhi. This gurdwara is dedicated to the first Sikh Guru, Guru Nanak Dev. The gurdwara was built at the site of the garden where Guru Nanak Dev camped when he visited Delhi in 1505.

GURDWARA PAONTA SAHIB is located in Himachal Pradesh and marks the place where Guru Gobind Singh stayed on the banks of River Yamuna.

GURDWARA PARIVAR VICHORA marks the place where Guru Gobind Singh separated from his mother Mata Gujri and young Sahibzadas, after an attack by the Mughal army.

GURDWARA PATALPURI is the place where ashes of Guru Hargobind in 1644 as well as Guru Har Rai in 1661 were cremated. The ashes of Guru Harkrishan were brought from Delhi and immersed here in 1664 as well.

GURDWARA PATSHAHI DASVIN, in Kurukshetra marks the place of visit of the Guru.

GURDWARA PATSHAHI DASVIN-GURUSAR marks the place where the tenth Sikh Guru, Sri Gobind Singh visited the place and stayed on his way from Dina in Moga.

GURDWARA PATTI SAHIB is located near Gurdwara Nankana Sahib in Pakistan. It is where Guru Nanak learnt the first alphabets of his life.

212

GURDWARA PEHLI PATSHAHI in Kurukshetra, Haryana, marks the place where Guru Nanak preached against superstitious practises.

GURDWARA PEHLI PATSHAHI, Pehowa is the place where Guru Nanak Dev meditated and preached people for a long time.

On the enthronement of Guru Arjan, a large sangat of tired and hungry devotees from Kabul wanting a glimpse of Guru Nanak camped at this spot where GURDWARA PIPLI SAHIB is built. On hearing their plight, Guru Angad asked his wife Mata Ganga to prepare food, which the Guru carried on his head to the camping site and tended to the old and tired travellers.

GURDWARA QILA FATEHGARH SAHIB in Anandpur Sahib, was built by Guru Gobind Singh to defend the city. It was during the construction of the fort that Sahibzada Fateh Singh was born, hence the name Fatehgarh.

GURDWARA RAKAB GANJ is a historic gurdwara near the Parliament House in New Delhi. It was built in 1783 by the Sikh military leader Baghel Singh to mark the site of cremation of the ninth Sikh Guru, Guru Tegh Bahadur.

GURDWARA SANGAT SAHIB: The treasure brought from Mal Tekri was brought here to be distributed among the Sikh warriors by Guru Gobind Singh. The shield used to distribute the treasure is preserved here.

GURDWARA SAT SANG SAHIB marks the place in Ambala where Bhai Jaita stopped with the severed head of Guru Tegh Bahadur on his way to Anandpur to meet Guru Gobind Singh.

GURDWARA SHAHEED BABA DEEP SINGH commemorates the martyrdom of Baba Deep Singh, who fought till his last breath to free the Durbar Sahib from the Afghan invaders.

GURDWARA SHAHIDI ASTHAAN BABA BANDA SINGH BAHADUR in Mehrauli is where Banda Bahadur took over the military leadership of the Sikhs after the death of Guru Gobind Singh. He, along with his four-year-old son and 40 Sikhs, was tortured to death by the Mughals here.

GURDWARA SHAHID GANJ is situated near Fateh Garh Sahib and marks the place where 40 cartload heads of the Sikhs, killed by the Mughal army, were cremated.

GURDWARA SHEESH MAHAL is located in the city of Kiratpur. It is the birthplace of Shri Har Rai Sahib and Guru Harkishan Sahib.

GURDWARA SHIKAR GHAT SAHIB is located on a low hill close to the river bank, close to Takhat Hazur Sahib. It is associated with Guru Gobind Singh, who used to visit this place for shikar.

GURDWARA SIS GANJ SAHIB was constructed in 1783 to commemorate the martyrdom of the 9th Guru, Guru Tegh Bahadur. This gurdwara in Chandni Chowk, Delhi, marks the site at which the Guru was beheaded on the orders of the Mughal Emperor Aurangzeb on 11 November 1675 for refusing to convert to Islam.

GURDWARA SIS GANJ SAHIB, Tarori, Haryana marks the place where Bhai Jaita, who was carrying the severed head of Guru Tegh Bahadur to Guru Gobind Singh at Anandpur, rested.

GURDWARA SISGANJ ANANDPUR marks the place where the severed head of Guru Tegh Bahadur was cremated after his execution in Delhi in 1675.

GURDWARA SRI DAMDAMA SAHIB situated in village Raqba in Ludhiana, marks the place where Guru Hargobind came while returning from Nanakmatta Sahib.

213

GURDWARA SRI BALA SAHIB is situated on the Ring road in Delhi which was once the bank of River Yamuna. Guru Harkrishan when afflicted with small pox, asked his followers to take him to an isolated location from the city. The Guru's last rites were performed here.

GURDWARA SRI TARN TARAN SAHIB was established by the fifth guru, Guru Arjan Dev, in the city of Tarn Taran. The site has the distinction of having the largest sarovar (water pond) of all the gurdwaras.

GURDWARA THAM SAHIB, located in Jalandhar district, marks the place where Guru Arjan stuck his walking stick in the ground and declared that the faith will get support from here.

GURDWARA TRIBENI SAHIB celebrates the visit of three Gurus, Guru Nanak, Guru Hargobind and Guru Gobind.

GURDWARA GURU NANAK JHIRA SAHIB is situated in Bidar, Karnataka. Bidar is long associated with Sikhism as Bhai Sahib Singh, one of the Panj Pyare (five beloved ones), who offered to sacrifice their heads and were later baptized as the first members of the Khalsa, belonged here.

GURDWARA SRI GURU TEGH BAHADUR SAHIB in Dhubri, Assam on the banks of Brahmaputra. Guru Nanak Dev visited Dubri in 1505 AD when he travelled from Dhaka to Assam. Later, the 9th Guru established this gurdwara in the 17th century.

GURDWARA SRI GURU NANAK DHAM RAMESHWARAM was constructed to commemorate the visit of the first Sikh guru, Guru Nanak, to Rameswaram, c. 1511.

GURDWARA SINGH SABHA, Pushkar or Pushkar Raj, a temple town around a natural lake, is 13 kms from Ajmer. Pushkar was visited by Guru Nanak Dev and Guru Gobind Singh. The shrine commemorating the former Guru's visit was earlier called Guru Nanak Dharmsala.

ACKNOWLEDGEMENTS

We acknowledge special thanks to Dr. Mohinder Singh, Dr. Amrik Singh and Dr. J.S. Neki of National Institute of Panjab Studies, who constantly guided us through the project.

SGPC for permission to photograph inside Harmandir Sahib, Toshakhana and Akal Takhat, Amritsar. Takhat Keshgarh Sahib, Anandpur; Takhat Damdama Sahib, Talwandi Sabo; Takhat Patna Sahib, Patna and Takhat Hazur Sahib, Nanded.

National Museum, New Delhi and National Archives of India, New Delhi

Punjab State Museum, Amritsar

Sikh Regimental Centre, Ramgarh
Delhi Gurdwara Prabandhak Committee
Victoria & Albert Museum, London

We also acknowledge invaluable cooperation from families, who are the custodians of the heritage of the Sikh Gurus and royalty for allowing us to photograph the treasure: Capt. Amarinder Singh, Patiala; The Bagrian family at Qila Bagrian; The Sangha family of Drolli Bhai Ki; Family of Mai Desan; Chak Fateh Singhwala family of Bhai Rupa, Village Bhai Rupa; Family of Bhai Dalla, Talwandi Sabo; Sodhi family of Guru Har Sahai; Lahore Museum for allowing photography of Princess Bamba Collection

Soldiers of Indian Army's Sikh Regimental Centre and Punjab Regiments take an oath as a granthi carries Guru Granth Sahib during a parade.

© Roli Books 2019

Published in India by Roli Books
M-75, Greater Kailash-II Market
New Delhi-110 048, India
Ph: ++91-11-40682000
E-mail: info@rolibooks.com
Website: www.rolibooks.com

ISBN: 978-81-939846-0-4

Design: Sneha Pamneja
Editor: Neelam Narula
Layout: Naresh L. Mondal
Pre-press: Jyoti Dey

Printed and bound in China